# PRAISE FOR TOM RANDLE

*"I have had the pleasure of serving as the immediate past Chair of the Board on Sarasota Coastal Credit Union's Board of Directors with Tom serving as the CEO. Tom has an engaging personal style that enables him to interact effectively with employees, members and potential partners within the community. Tom met the expected parameters of his job as the CEO and did so for 20 years. I volunteered to write this recommendation for Tom because I am very grateful for his contributions to Sarasota Coastal and to the credit union philosophy and very confident that he has the intelligence, work ethic and communications skills to add value wherever he chooses to work. Tom, I know this is very hard and I appreciate your professionalism through this process. And, I meant what I said during the toast...you have demonstrated that you are a great leader and it shows in the loyalty and support of everyone around you...I feel slighted that I didn't get to work with you for the entire 20 years, but I am really glad that I was able to get to know you over the last few years. It has been my honor too. Thanks for all you are doing!"*
--- **Janet Cantees**, Chair of the Board of Directors, Sarasota Coastal Credit Union


*"I've known Tom Randle for all my 20 years here at CUES. He was a board member for six years and Chairman for one of those. I find him to be a man of integrity and competence who I would want my children to work for and learn from. My highest recommendation. He's a natural CEO and marginal golfer (like me - the latter, not the former)."*
--- **Fred Johnson**, CEO, Credit Union Executives Society

*"Tom is a results oriented chief executive with exceptional leadership and motivational skills. He is a terrific communicator, yet listens carefully and is not afraid to entertain divergent points of view. He has a gifted analytical mind, one terrific sense of humor and is a pleasure to work with. Tom is not only a supportive, fair and ethical business partner; he is truly one of the good guys. I recommend him without hesitation or qualification!"*
--- **Bill Goldberg**, President, Auto Advisor Services, LLC


*"I was anticipating a message from you with regard to the merger and how it will affect you. Now that I know, I am deeply saddened to learn that the merger will end your leadership of SCCU. I, as well as past and present members of the Board, are fully cognizant of the unprecedented emergence of our CU to the high level of growth that resulted due to your expert leadership. It is an unfitting end to your role as CEO. I do not understand the attitude of the CU who will be taking over our CU. Your presence will be missed by all who have worked with you. I feel certain that all of the management team are going to miss your presence. Please feel free to use my name as a long-time Board member to serve as a reference to recommend you as a CEO of any CU that is looking for solid and experienced leadership. I shall always remember the good times we had at CU conventions and the golf outings. I really miss those times. I do hope you and Mary will find happiness wherever you relocate. Thanks for the memories and for all you did for our Credit Union."*
--- **Russ Brown**, past Director, Sarasota Coastal Credit Union

*"Tom Randle was the National CUES president for some time, during which CUES strived to focus on the professional development of members, and not so much in competition with Leagues and CUNA's. He is a big picture individual, has been very active, especially in the political action arena, and I might add effective, (which I wish we could say about all CU folks), and has most recently, been a Florida League Board member, and a Florida Credit Union Foundation Trustee. He was a strong advocate for the consolidation of the Florida and Alabama Leagues. I personally am convinced that he would make a Great League President! He is a true "outside the box" thinker. Tom's credit union, of which he was CEO, got caught up, victimized, actually, by the housing collapse in West Florida. Beyond that, his Credit Union was always healthy, and very politically active, as well as within their local community. He is a quality individual."*

--- **Guy Hood**, Florida Credit Union League, Inc. (retired)


*"Tom is an experienced leader, not just in his professional endeavors but also in life. Tom brings his lifelong experiences in the military, as an executive, and as a community leader to his relationships. He balances the drive for success with the quality of life. This characteristic is exhibited by Tom in all his accomplishments. Tom focuses on 'what counts'. If you are looking for someone who understands what is needed to get the job done and knows how to complete the job, then you should talk to Tom. He can help you achieve success with his experience, skills and ability to communicate what you need to be successful."*

--- **Catherine Bruder**, Shareholder at Doeren Mayhew

# NOTE FROM THE AUTHOR

I have recreated events, locales and conversations from my memories of them. In order to maintain anonymity for those who asked that I do so, I have changed the names of some individuals and places and changed identifying characteristics and details such as physical properties, occupations and places of residence.

The information contained within this book is strictly for educational purposes. If you wish to apply the ideas I have shared, you take full responsibility for your actions and the results.

I have made every effort to ensure the accuracy of the information within this book at the time of publication. I do not assume and hereby disclaim any liability to any party for any loss, damage, or disruption caused by errors or omissions, whether such errors or omissions result from accident, negligence, or any other cause.

Tom Randle
Sarasota, FL and Clayton, GA
April 2017

# SHOULDERING THE COST

## One Credit Union CEO's Take
## on the
## Great Banking Collapse of 2008

By

## Tom Randle

First Electronic Edition: May 2017
First Print Edition: September 2017

# TABLE OF CONTENTS

# FOREWORD

*"The best and most beautiful things in the world cannot be seen or even touched, but just felt in the heart."* --- Helen Keller

I was encouraged to write this book by some who said it would serve as a record of the most turbulent time in the credit union movement and financial services industry since the Great Depression. I also felt there needed to be a discussion of leadership by the people and agencies that, including myself, performed miserably during the time leading up to the merger that destroyed an organization (founded in 1953) that was the one of the largest non-profits on the southwest coast of Florida. The merger caused my unemployment and that of dozens of my co-workers. Many of us lost our homes. Our marriages. And many have remained unemployed or under-employed for years.

My heart says a plain speaking description that chronicles the loss of honor, exposes overzealousness and shines a light on indifference should be shared as a learning experience. To do nothing leaves undone the lessons to be learned from the downfall and failure of persons and agencies entrusted to protect.

This is my truth. If there is any doubt as to my purpose for telling this story, it is this...

You may think I'm a self-righteous hypocrite. But, I do not agree. At no point throughout this account do I ignore my own faults and failures. I am so far from perfect, as you'll see.

By sharing this story with you, I can finally forgive those involved, and myself.

# PROLOGUE

*"Grief is like the ocean; it comes on waves ebbing and flowing. Sometimes the water is calm, and sometimes it is overwhelming. All we can do is learn to swim."* --- Vicki Harrison

L ove and laughter used to live in this home. Now, it's empty.

I remember thinking this on Father's Day 2010 when my wife and I felt forced to sell our home in Sarasota, Florida and were moving to rural NE Georgia facing an uncertain future. My heart no longer resided in my chest. It resided in my shoes taking a crushing blow with each step I took toward what would no longer be my front door.

The last three years had been bad, really bad. The Great Recession, which started in December 2007, according to the "experts," began a lot earlier in S.W. Florida. Those same "experts" claimed it was over, but there was still pain throughout the country caused by high unemployment and the loss of real estate values. Moreover, it was pain that I knew all-too-well and was still struggling to overcome each and every day.

I had no job, or prospects for one, and to say that I was angry and resentful would not come close to covering the sharp-edge cutting through my soul.

Not knowing that our world was going to crash even more, my wife and I had purchased a mountain home with the plan to work another six or so years. Once we retired, we'd use the mountain house for vacations and live there in the summers. The decision to sell our Florida house was entirely an economic one. We could no longer afford to live there full-time.

After 39 years of serving and helping others—the last 25 years as a Credit Union CEO, I was cast off. What had been my calling and never just a job to me was taken away. I am not the first, nor the last, to lose a job. And this is not a sob story. It is a first-hand account of the failure of leadership at many levels. I hope that you will, as I have, take the lessons to be learned from this to your heart.

The experiences and actions taken by banking regulators were not unique to me and my credit union. Hundreds, perhaps thousands, of other Credit Union CEO's went through comparable treatment.

Some contributors to this book provided their own experiences with the request that their identity not be disclosed as they are still employed in the credit union movement and fear retaliation. Others asked that their names be attributed with a bit of incitement.

I have been advised by many in the industry that I am taking on the biggest machines I can take on and warned that they play dirty. The big machines I'm referring to are the federal and state regulatory systems. They can literally ban a person for life from working in a financial institution. They can issue a Letter of Understanding (LUA) or worse, a Document of Resolution (DOR), which compels a board of directors to comply with whatever action the regulators deem is needed to protect the deposit insurance fund, including blocking or granting preapproval of the hiring of executives.

Be not fooled. The federal and state regulatory agencies do not give a shit about you, your credit union or bank, its employees, your board of directors or your members (customers). It's George Orwell's 1984 all over again.

For this story to contain verifiable references and sources for each citation, it would require the participation of persons and agencies that are unwilling to do so. I accept the fact that we all have First Amendment Rights, and this book does cast big shadows on the character, intelligence and capability of high-ranking people. I, of all people, understand that there is nothing more devastating to a person's soul than a false accusation. And I assure you, I make no false accusations in this book. It's the truth…as ugly as it is.

The terms regulator and examiner are odious in this context. The reality is that those pejorative terms describe what happened to the entire credit union movement. I once believed that Credit Union CEO's, Directors and Examiners were the people in the white hats. It never crossed my mind back then that those persons could be much more than economical with the truth.

Believing at all times that I was in communication with honorable persons; meticulous logs of every conversation or event were not maintained. There were witnesses to almost all incidents. On more than one occasion, a recording was made of the exit interviews and copies were provided to the examiners present. Often, our attorney was present or participated by conference call.

The persons and agencies that had a role in my experiences are living and can corroborate the facts. But do not expect that they will. These are incidents of situational ethics, intentional harm and pretty lies. I have no illusions that they will now or ever demonstrate honorableness, integrity or principles.

My story is an illustration of how ethics, honor, and leadership are fundamentally missing in the regulatory system and in some credit unions. My intent is not to demonize or vilify. My intent is to show that undesirable and unethical behaviors destroyed and continue to destroy not only our banking and financial systems but also careers and lives.

Could the message be delivered with a more sensitive approach? Perhaps. But this is not an exit interview conducted by a seasoned human resources director, trained to make or give a dire situation a positive spin. It is a story of a massive collision of egos in which none of the parties handle themselves with distinction, including, and most importantly, myself.

When leaders attain the lofty position of a Paragon of Trust, the fall is life-threatening. There is a quote in Genesis 5:24: "Enoch walked with the Lord; and then he was no more, for God took him." The most wonderful interpretation I have heard of that passage is attributed to Rev. Dr. W. Frank Harrington, Senior Pastor, Peachtree Presbyterian Church Atlanta. He summed it up as: "Every day Enoch walked with God and God walked with Enoch. Each day they walked a little further together until one day they walked so far that God said to Enoch, 'We are closer to my house than yours...why don't you come home with me?'"

Banking and Financial Leaders have walked so far away from honor and integrity that perhaps all that is left to do is put the system to rest and begin anew. The pendulum has swung so far that regaining integrity and public trust may not be attainable.

# INTRODUCTION

*"Right is not right; so is not so. If right were really right, it would differ so clearly from not right that there would be no need for argument. If so were really so, it would differ so clearly from not so that there would be no need for argument. Forget the years; forget distinctions. Leap into the boundless and make it your home."* --- Chuang-Tzu

Long ago, I decided to leave a record on the subjects of honor and integrity for my children. Honor and integrity are ingrained in me. Intrinsically, we know honor and integrity, and we know when we see it shattered.

For me, the journey began in the 11th grade, when I chose to marry my sweetheart, who I met when we were both 15 years old. I did it for love, a sense of duty and honor, and because she was pregnant. It was not a sensible choice, but it produced a daughter and son I love more than life itself. Being under legal age, I needed my mother's consent to marry. She reluctantly agreed upon the condition that I join the U.S. Army, which also required her consent.

The U.S. Army offered me lessons on integrity, accountability, teamwork and caring about others. My military experience left an indelible imprint and has served as a guide and source of inspiration. I am reminded often that I have been in worse situations.

I married at age 17 and within 30 days, I was off to basic training, AIT, then stationed away from my child bride and about-to-be-born daughter. When I was stationed in Germany, we were reunited for a few months where my daughter had her first birthday, and we were together sporadically thereafter whenever I came home on leave.

I spent what should have been the rest of my high school days in Vietnam (from February 1969-February 1970). In fact, I left Vietnam on my 20th birthday and got to celebrate it twice as we crossed the international dateline on the return trip.

I was an SP-5 in the Corps of Engineers, operating in IV Corp, South Vietnam. While in Vietnam, the letters from my wife stopped coming. That is never a good thing. All GI's know that the letters from home keep us going. Eventually, divorce papers arrived. I refused to sign them and tried to be approved for leave to go back to Florida and take care of my problems and my daughter.

Wisely, the company commander did not approve my leave request. If I went home, he said, I would simply kill both my wife and her US Navy lover from Punta Gorda, Florida, neither of which would serve me well. Thanks go to God for wiser men in charge.

In Basic Training, the drill instructors used a song to mark cadence as we marched: "Jody's got your girl and gone, sound off." Well, Jody came in the form of a sailor. However, I did refuse to sign off on the divorce and came home in February 1970 to find my wife and daughter hiding in Hollywood, Florida and Jody on a ship in the Mediterranean.

Apparently, my wife and mother had called the Red Cross to ask where I was and learned I had been discharged two weeks earlier. Unknown to them, I was wandering the country attempting to drain out the jungle blood and make sense of my year in Vietnam, before finding them. They had watched too many movies and assumed I was coming home with an M-60 machine gun, so my wife took our daughter and retreated to her biological father's home in Hollywood, Florida.

According to published articles and conversations with my comrades in arms, our land clearing units had 47 killed in action and 800 wounded in Vietnam. Unbeknownst to most of us, there was a bounty on our heads by the North Vietnamese Army because our Rome Plows, specially equipped Caterpillar D-7 tractors retrofitted with parts manufactured in Rome, Georgia, destroyed ground cover and disrupted troop and supply routes. Collectively, all land clearing units destroyed an area equal to the size of the state of Connecticut. What we did not push over was sprayed with Agent Orange (AO), a defoliant. Most "Jungle Eaters" were sprayed with AO and deal with ongoing health issues 45 plus years later.

The difference between my Vietnam days and my life as a Credit Union CEO was that in Vietnam, I knew others were trying to do me harm, and I to them…a very straightforward relationship. In the financial industry, the enemy doesn't always reveal themselves, or they come in disguise.

Below is a letter from our Battalion Commander…

EGEB-CO                                                    21 January 1970

SUBJECT: Commendation


Officers and Men
60th Engineer Company (LC)
AFO 96491


Now that the smoke has cleared a bit and the story of your ordeal on 18
January has emerged, I would like to transmit to you a few of my thoughts.

Having the oldest traditions in land clearing, the 60th has developed over
the past year the reputation as a renegade outfit. There was a time when
Long Birh Post shuddered at the mere thought of the 60th coming in on stand
down. Our neighbors across the "ditch" often found it necessary to go on
Red Alert.

I suppose that more than any other company, the 60th is responsible for
establishing the flamboyant spirit of land clearers. To the best of my
knowledge, your company has never been on an easy operation and probably
never will go on one. I think this accounts for the "let-it-all-hang-
out" attitude which has been passed on from old-timer to newcomer since
the days of the 27th Land Clearing Team—the original Jungle Eaters.

While this kind of spirit can be a decided pain in the ass to me while you're
in garrison, it is this same spirit that has carried you through the toughest
operations any land clearing unit has ever faced. And it is the spirit that
was remarkably in evidence on the evening of 18 January. I have never in my
life encountered a company of officers and men so completely dedicated to one
another. I am especially impressed with how the officers of your company
refer to their men in their casual conversations with me. I doubt if enlisted
men anywhere have such total respect from their officers.

I am extremely sorry for the losses you experienced, but I am certain that
the enemy will pay a heavy price for that attack. Nobody—friend or foe—
screws over the 60th without coming up losers. That's your tradition and
that's the way its going to be. In visiting your buddies in the hospital,
General Dillard, the CO of Engineer Troops, was deeply moved by the morale
and spirit that these men have. I must say that it is very hard to visit
these men without choking up a bit. They're beautiful.

I wish to thank each of you for your courage, your dedication, and your Spirit.
Being associated with you is the greatest privilige I will ever have.

                                        You're beautiful,

                                        PAUL C DRISCOLL
                                        LTC, CE
                                        Commanding

~ 8 ~

I suppose for some of you that letter and $0.85 will get you a senior coffee at McDonald's. But to me, it means so much more. If there is a point to all this, it's that I found the Army and being yelled at, being underpaid, cold, shot at and under duress 24/7 to be a good way for an irresponsible teenager to learn important life lessons not readily available to all.

On several occasions throughout the process of writing of this book, my coach posed this question: "What were you feeling during this time?"

For all of you big, old hairy-legged men reading this, you know we manly men do not like discussions that begin with "tell me what you are feeling." But then it hit me. If I am to tell my story, and tell it authentically, I am obliged to share with you an answer to her question.

The feeling I had at that time in my life was that my intestines were being removed by the propeller of an outboard motor while I watched. There was an actual physical pain in my guts and nuts that I can still feel 48 years later.

I wrote about my feelings at that time in a letter to a woman who used to babysit me and my sister when were children in Greensboro, North Carolina, where we lived until age 13. When she passed away, I attended her service and one of her daughters returned to me several of the letters I had written to her mom during my time in Vietnam. On a father-daughter trip to Washington, DC while seated at the base of The Wall, I gave those letters to my adult daughter. I told her that the contents of the letters cast aspersions upon her mother, and I was sorry for that. I told her to keep them or destroy them as she wished.

How did I feel many years later when the Great Banking Collapse ground my organization and me into dust? When the state and federal examiners behaved like petulant children? When my peers lied to me throughout the merger negotiations that I initiated? When most of my beloved employees were laid off and I was, at age 59, unemployed? When not one of my friends from 29 years of working together in credit unions called me?

I felt exactly as I did at age 19 when I received my divorce papers in Vietnam.

After two weeks of wandering aimlessly upon my return from Vietnam, I arrived in Jacksonville, and my father-in-law and two of my brothers-in-law picked me up at the airport. On the way to their home (the two boys were still in high school), my father-in-law, who wrote to me regularly in Vietnam and was the nearest I had to a father, told me where my wife and child were and loaned me his car to go get them. I drove to Hollywood, Florida to retrieve my wife and child and then back to Jacksonville to begin a life.

I had been discharged from active duty for just three weeks and was now living with my wife's mother and stepdad. I received a phone call from a neighbor of my mom and stepdad letting me know Mom wasn't well. But I didn't know what to believe. My mother was a hypochondriac and a drama queen. I spoke with her briefly by phone and promised to come see her soon. I needed to stay where I was for a while to reconnect with my wife and daughter and get my head straight.

Mom died at home the next day at age 42. After I left for Vietnam, I never saw her alive again. The autopsy said it was an accidental overdose of prescription drugs and kidney failure. So, three weeks after getting home from Vietnam, I identified my mother's body on a slab at the Duval County, Florida morgue.

I wasn't able to shed a tear. It was just another dead body.

I made arrangements and Mom was buried in a closed casket and is interred at Jacksonville Beach, near another son she gave birth to who died of SIDS.

I was a Vietnam vet, with a child, but no job and a very shaky marriage based upon infidelity and mistrust. At 20-years-old, I had my first midlife crisis. That effectively closed one chapter of my life, and I made myself move on.

I know now, looking back, that the betrayal of my wife, loss of my mother, the chaos of Vietnam, the public scorn with which I and all vets were treated in those days, and my stepdad getting remarried quickly and having another slew of children, all played a part in my formation of values and personal code of honor. I could have gone a dark way, very, very easily.

I came home to a nation that spit upon its veterans and showed a total lack of respect and support for my generation. I got mad in 1970, and never got over it.

After my mother passed away, my stepdad married a mean, nasty woman who had children of her own. Those children at some point had been removed from her care by Florida Department of Children and Families (DFCS) for neglect, abuse or abandonment. I do not know the specifics.

My half-brother, who is 12 years my junior, was 7 when our mother died and has little recall of her. My stepdad's new wife beat my little brother to the point that there were bruises and welts seen by my sister, who I encouraged to call the police. The authorities removed our brother and placed him in the care of a Catholic home off Arlington Expressway, Jacksonville, Florida.

I went to see him on a Sunday, the only visiting hours allowed, and was appalled. A scene from Oliver Twist comes to mind. Granted, I barely knew him, as I had left home at age 17 when he was 4, but blood is thicker than water and my sense of duty and honor took charge. I picked him up and walked out the door of that home with Nuns running after me saying I couldn't do that.

About an hour later, the Jacksonville Sherriff's Office was at my door. We had a tense conversation through the slightly ajar door and security chain. The officer got a Justice of the Peace to call me, and I spoke with her. She granted me temporary custody, pending a hearing, in lieu of having me arrested.

At the hearing, my stepdad, his new wife, the DFCS and a bunch of lawyers showed up. The judge heard my plea not to put my little brother into foster care as I had a job by now and a home and could care for him. I was able to get Social Security Survivor's benefits for him from Mom's account and enrolled him into the 4th grade. He and my daughter played together, and my son was born later that year.

My son was born in February 1972, which increased our family to five persons. I was 22. We lived in government-subsidized housing under a FHA 235 program. I worked, went to college on the GI Bill, and moonlighted as a lifeguard at the housing development pool. Life was good.

DFCS made unannounced visits to oversee the care of my brother. On one visit, not long after my son was born, DFCS came. I was at work. My wife told the DFCS caseworker that caring for my little brother, on top of a newborn child and a four ½ year old daughter, was too much on her.

When I came home that afternoon from work and night classes at the community college, my brother was gone. He had been taken into custody by DFCS. A hearing was scheduled to determine where he would be placed. It was clear that it would not be with me.

I went to that hearing without legal counsel, under the assumption that I had done the right things and was dealing with honorable persons in the juvenile justice system. The judge did not award custody to my stepdad, my brother's birth father and his new wife, because of her history with DFCS. So, my little brother was placed into foster care for a number of years. (My career caused me to move outside Jacksonville, so I was not eligible to gain custody of him. My sister was finally able to get our little brother out of foster care and raised him through high school.)

That day in the courtroom, I came perilously close to serious jail time. The judge was a very patient man and waived off the officers. I asked him to do one thing for me. And that was to bring my little brother into the courtroom and explain to him that I was not abandoning him. He did so, and for that, I am thankful. I tried to act with duty and honor, but it didn't seem to be enough.

That experience soured me towards DFCS, foster care and the juvenile justice system, Today, I have been a CASA/Guardian Ad Litem for over five years, largely to advocate for children who, like my little brother, cannot speak for themselves in court.

If you asked me what happened to my first marriage, it boils down to this...lack of trust and honor. The mother of my children had an affair with a sailor while I was in Vietnam, filed for divorce and gave away my brother. Many years after we were divorced, she called me and apologized for what happened with my brother and for not understanding the consequences of my experiences in Vietnam. Fool me once, shame on you; fool me twice, shame on me; there wouldn't be a third time.

I remained married to the mother of my children for 16 years. We divorced in 1983, and I married the woman I lovingly call "the redhead" in December 1985. Wonderful things do happen to those who wait.

The reason I'm sharing my past is it's those experiences that taught me personal accountability...that our actions are controllable and are key success factors in life. Whether

Vietnam was the root cause or not, the fact is, I came home a changed man. A man-child who at age 20, after nearly three years of active duty, could not vote or buy a beer.

The mother of my children, may God rest her soul, caught the blunt of an angry husband who drank too much, swore too much and was a lousy husband. PTSD was not a term in use at that time. Manly men held it in and sucked it up, as our fathers had done after WWII and Korea.

# PART I: A CHECK OF THE ENVIRONMENT

*"The only time you should ever look back, is to see how far you've come."* --- Author Unknown

According to the Financial Times (August 9, 2007), Sarasota, Florida was at the center of the United States housing bust. I did not need to read it in the Financial Times; I was in the center of that bust as the CEO of Sarasota Coastal Credit Union.

No documentation lenders and speculators/flippers drove up prices and fueled unbridled lending in first mortgages and home equity loans (HELOC) with many funded at 125% of the appraised value. The proceeds were used to fund risk-taking by homeowners and lenders willing to bet that prices would continue to rise as they had from 2002-2007.

Homeowners used their homes as an ATM. I watched people refinance their primary residence six times. Most spent the money on vacations. Others bought houses to flip. Not one of them saved or reinvested in property improvements of their primary home.

Florida was the canary in the coalmine and unemployment rates in Sarasota hit 13.5%. Adjusted for persons no longer looking or self-employed it was 20%. Only Detroit had a higher number. Residential real estate prices plummeted as much as 60%. The average number of listings in the Sarasota MLS before the bust was 2,400 properties. In June 2008, that number was down to 1,600, but by December 2008, it increased to 4,800. By May 2011, there were over 11,000 properties for sale in the Sarasota MLS.

Our home sold in June 2010, after only eight months on the market, for 50% of the appraised value just two years earlier. Sitting on a depreciating asset hastened our acceptance of the only solid offer we received.

*Note: For a deeper appreciation of the situation and decision-making, check out* The Florida Financial Hurricane: A Credit Union Risk Management Case Study, *Franck Schuurmans, PhD (Apr 15, 2011), Filene Research Institute. I was a contributing author in the study, and the credit union used as the case study was the one of which I was CEO. Dr. Schuurmans was our facilitator when we undertook scenario vs. strategic planning. His published study walks the reader through the process.*

The entire country was in a weak economy and experiencing an epic collapse in housing with an estimated 800,000 foreclosures by or in 2011 alone. Keep in mind, this is the context for the time period well after the "experts" claimed the Great Recession had ended (May-June, 2009). In actuality, it was the worst credit crisis since the Great Depression. Consumers were pinched, and borrowing had all but stopped as consumers built up savings accounts in an abundance of caution. 46,000 jobs were lost in Sarasota and Manatee Counties, Florida.

Nationally, by July 2011, there were 13.9 million unemployed persons and the unemployment rate was 9.1%. Again...this is nearly two years after the recession was officially said to have ended. We still had almost 14 million people out of work and 45 million on food stamps. Over 6 million were unemployed more than 27 weeks. Add to that dismal news, the global economy, the U.S. stock markets, and the downgrade of the U.S. credit rating and that of several major banks.

There were 58 bank failures in the United States through July 2011 and 9 of those (15.5%) were in Florida. The 57th failure and 9th in Florida was Landmark Bank, Sarasota, July 2011.

The $275 million asset community bank cost the FDIC $34.4 million and had a 1-star Bankrate.com rating and 0-star at Bauer Financial. The former CEO once said that the growth of his bank had been impeded by our credit union. Really?! The bank reached assets of $275 million in about 6 years, while our credit union required 56 years to reach $235 million.

Nationwide, 9 credit unions were forced into conservatorship by NCUA (National Credit Union Administration) in 2011. Bank of America eliminated 6,000 positions and announced plans to cut another 30,000 positions as it struggled to respond to the economic conditions.

On July 18, 2011, The Credit Union Journal reported that Southwest Corporate Federal Credit Union released its second quarter 2011 CEO Confidence Survey, and the report showed confidence among credit union CEOs declined again and was near a record low as the economic recovery was slow to take hold. In the face of overwhelming evidence that the country was gripped in its worst recession in 80 years, that the current economic crisis was deeper than first thought and had lasted longer than anyone could have imagined, regulatory agencies remain inadequately informed and unable to take right action.

Paradise can be an illusion. Numerous, intelligent people ignored the warning signs. Siesta Key, Lido Beach, St. Armand's Circle, Longboat Key and Ringling Bros. conjure images of white sand beaches, palm trees, blue gulf waters and wealth. In 2011, Stephen P. "Dr. Beach" Leatherman, once again selected Siesta Key as the #1 beach. The area has movie and rock stars, celebrities, rich Europeans and snowbirds from Ohio and Illinois who never turn off the left turn signal on their Cadillacs.

Housing had been increasing in double-digit values in the run up to 2007. The construction and tourism industries plus the arts and amenities of the beaches and museums were strong. So much so that Ritz Carlton opened a Sarasota location, and there were multi-million dollar projects planned and permitted along the bay front by international organizations.

The local mullet wrap (the Sarasota Herald-Tribune and its employees were in our credit union's field of membership) reported that Neiman Marcus and other luxury retailers were soon to join Sak's. Shopping malls were renovated, and long-term plans were to keep expanding indefinitely. A world-class rowing facility was being planned.

Realtors were making substantial commissions. An acquaintance of mine obtained a real estate license, got one referral and made one million dollars in commissions in a month. Even conservative people were buying and flipping houses. It was easy to make money in that environment, and the lure for more was insatiable.

Before the Great Recession, unemployment had been as low as 3%, making recruitment of qualified employees challenging. There was opportunity everywhere, and when potential employees have so many options, they are in a position to negotiate. Add to that challenge the high cost of living and housing in Sarasota, which drove salaries and benefits. Signing bonuses became a normal part of attracting employees to come to work for us.

In those years, banks were being chartered in record numbers, and credit unions were opening branches in Sarasota from as far away as Miami and Tampa. Everybody was doing great, growing, making money and all did so under the supervision of their boards, examiners, and within the laws and regulations of the state and federal examiners.

Right action, honor and integrity are timeless and take measure of one's character. The situational lapses of right action, honor and integrity throughout the banking and financial industry before, during and after the 2008 Collapse represent a variation in one's character that cannot be attributed solely to economic conditions; they are due to our human condition.

# Chapter 1: Adding a Few Layers of Context

*"First, things are seen plainer after the events have occurred; second, that the most confident critics are generally those who know the least about the matter criticized."* --- Ulysses S. Grant

This was not the first real estate crisis in Florida, and it will not be the last. Swampland and hucksters have been in Florida for 150 years.

Persons that repeatedly took cash out or bought too much house with nothing down found themselves "upside down". We called it "jingle mail" as we received the keys to the abandoned houses in the mail when the owner walked away from their legal and moral obligation.

The number of homeowners allowed to purchase more house than they could afford with little or nothing down has been substantially under-reported. If you want to know what fueled this housing crisis, and why your home's value dropped with it, just look out your kitchen window at your neighbor's home. They financed it via "liar loans" with nothing down, no income verification, no verified capacity to repay the debt, and did so with an adjustable rate mortgage that benefitted the mortgage broker.

When they walked away, the resulting foreclosure or short sale reduced your property value, too. You get to look at knee-high grass, a green swimming pool and vandalism of the property by the departing owners. It is common that the owners destroy the interior as they leave. That is especially so when renters, who may be current in their obligation, learn they are being evicted because their property owner, who accepted the rent each month, did not pay the mortgage company. That happened to my son, btw.

*\*\*\*Note: Watch the Oscar-winning movie The Big Short for a great look inside the housing bubble.*

Homeowners were allowed to default on their mortgage payments for years while remaining in the house, and the larger mortgages were the last to be foreclosed upon because the smaller mortgage balances were easier to sell. Big banks and lenders were swamped with workouts, and the backlog of volume created apathy with the mortgage holders. Frequently, they would not even take a call from the debtors until the mortgage was in arrears over 90 days. I knew people who remained in their home for 18 months without making any payments. The mortgage holders could not produce proof that they owned the mortgage, as the mortgages were packaged with others and sold to the secondary market.

All these factors combined to create unstable economic conditions of historic proportions and adversely affect almost all industries. Businesses were forced to close their doors and lay off staff in numbers not witnessed in many generations. Ultimately, my employer, too, succumbed to the pressure and did likewise.

For my family, I felt with the real estate market in full implosion, and more than 50% of our equity vaporized, the best decision was to move to a place with a much lower cost-of-living. Doing so was predicated on the expectation that I was an experienced, respected CEO in my industry and would land another position shortly.

We could have stayed in our Sarasota home. My wife had a 20 year job she loved, and I had accepted the position of interim-CEO, Sarasota Habitat for Humanity. I could have stayed there at 66% of my previous salary, but I could not secure another position remotely equal to the one I had lost.

An unintended consequence of this experience was that my wife resigned her 20 year position with a dental practice, left all her friends, workout buddies, executive home, familiar surroundings and followed me to rural NE Georgia. The redhead is resistant to change and was depressed for the better part of three years. The only jobs she could secure in the small mountain town were barista at Starbucks for eight months and then three years in the optical department of our Walmart.

Both honorable jobs and she enjoyed them. Still, it was a blow to my male psyche and to my heart to sit at home conducting job searches while my wife was working at Walmart.

It is worth noting here that, post-merger, the displaced staff in almost all cases never find jobs anywhere close to the salary they lost. Lifetime earnings, retirement and health care insurance are also affected.

I said to my loving, supportive wife that the experience caused me to lose my faith in God, and regretfully, that feeling lasted for a while.

In his book *Win at Losing*, Sam Weinman makes the case that failure can be used as fuel. The question, "Did you fail, or just lose?" is uncomfortable. Weinman suggests that failure implies fault; losing, however, may be beyond your control. Chances are that you did not fail…rather, you lost to someone better prepared or to someone who had information you didn't.

After 25 years as a Credit Union CEO, I can speak to feelings of failure...and to how it feels to lose, big-time. The 2008 Banking Collapse ended my career. The economic tsunami rolled over my entire organization due to mortgage losses created by big banks and mortgage lenders. In spite of the examiner stating that this was an economic crisis, and not a management event, I felt I was a failure. It's taken me many years to understand and accept that it was a loss beyond my control.

I disagree with Weinman, though, that "no pain, no gain" is a positive approach to life. Calling that phrase science-based and using terms like "post-traumatic growth" is dishonorable to anyone who suffers from PTSD and only serves to further embolden the type of people who seek safe places in clichés like this when things get messy and more than their feelings and egos are hurt.

Losing is debilitating. Even though learning from your losses is an opportunity for personal and professional growth, it's not a necessity to lose in order to gain. If you are consistently losing when it comes to your jobs, promotions, relationships or your health, then its time you did something very differently.

Realizing you've lost and not failed will alleviate stress and improve your well-being. Research has proven that. I had a Director who said stress was good. But, he was wrong. Unless you are an athlete who chooses to channel stress in short increments to sharpen your focus and improve performance, stress can kill you, literally.

Acknowledging your part in the experience is an important step. When you fail or lose, you often blame others. That's not productive, either. The problem is never external. Both the problem and the answer always lie within you. Yes. The problem is there outside of you. But, it's how you choose to deal with it that determines the overall impact on your life. You are the only one who can allow your outside influences and circumstances to crush your enthusiasm, motivation and desire and ability to do the honorable things you need to do to detach from the situation. There is value in making mistakes, on that I agree. But, if you continue to criticize yourself for past errors, you perpetuate the very behavior you want to change. To stop the cycle, you must take responsibility for your failures.

Failure is a state of mind. Unsuccessful people allow life's setbacks to discourage and defeat them. Successful people view setbacks as learning experiences and bounce back stronger…every time.

After more than 40 years of experience, it's my observation that people fail to achieve their dreams of an abundant, satisfying life and career when the arrogance of their egos gets in the way…not that they would admit it.

Leaders are not born. Leadership is learned. Everything, except intelligence, we acquire after birth. We are not born in God's image to be arrogant and devoid of integrity and ethics. Being a product of our past experiences is something all of us, as humans, have in common. That does not have to limit or define who or what we can become.

Beyond 25 years as a Credit Union CEO, I have my military experience and leadership roles in both for-profit and not-for-profit worlds, and I've served on numerous boards of directors as a volunteer, and continue to do so.

In all of these positions, I saw pride and self-conceit become limitations. Arrogance grows unchecked and becomes hubris, which stifles the qualities that we admire most such as empathy, passion, heart, feelings, admiration, reverence and wonder. Name one leader that you admire that does not now, or did when they were alive, possess these endearing qualities.

Like you, I have former friends, business associates and others with whom I crossed paths that I would have liked to slap silly...But they don't need my judgment. They are their own worst enemies.

As a certified business coach, I work exclusively with ethical, successful leaders who are prepared to make positive behavioral changes in themselves, their teams and their organizations. All my clients have come to a crossroad and acknowledge that in order to achieve work-life balance, something must change. It wakes them up at 2 am.

Whether the changes they need to make are mental, social, spiritual or family-related is unique to each individual; however, the changes they make always impact their family and career development.

All men and women who've left a mark on the world possessed courage. They faced the challenges in their life; they spoke out and had the courage of their convictions to back them up. Courage isn't inherited, either. You develop it by believing in yourself and adhering to your values and goals. Courage attracts others to follow, respect and support you.

"Courage," Sir Winston Churchill said, "is resistance to fear, mastery of fear --- not absence of fear...Courage is the first of human qualities...because it is the quality which guarantees all others."

Courage and confidence grows as you face challenges, set goals and strive to achieve them. Partner with a positive attitude, and it makes it almost impossible to fail. That doesn't mean those of us who live by these principles aren't afraid. We saddle up anyway and in doing so, inspire others.

I'm a leader who has shouldered the costs, and it's my duty to share my story to help facilitate the return of honor to the financial and banking system and to my life.

# Chapter 2: Going Down the Rabbit Hole

Not in my wildest dreams could I have predicted the Great Recession and very few did. No computer model forecast the depth, severity and impact it had. In the book *Sharing the American Dream, A Second Look* by the Credit Unions Executives Society (1995), I was a contributing author and wrote about embracing change and the future. One of my coaching clients shared with me that she had come across a copy and read it. She said everything I forecast in 1995 came to realization. I just didn't realize, at the time, how devastating the fall-out would be. To put into context what happened, it helps to first look back and identify the signs.

The run-up in consumer debt began ten years earlier in 1998. By 2007, the housing bubble burst in what are known as the Sand States...California, Arizona, Nevada and Florida. The recession, however, had been in effect for two plus years before the regulatory agencies acknowledged there was one. Note the following:

•It was a deep, long recession and had a double-dip that would be worse.
•The Wall Street Journal reported savings rates in the U.S. were at 75-year lows.
•Credit Unions did not act in a timely manner to cut deposit rates, leading to deposit (asset) growth. That reduced net worth ratios and Return on Average Assets (ROAA).

Exasperating the problem further, the National Credit Union Administration (NCUA) seized five Corporate CU's (Corporate credit unions function as a bank for credit unions by providing liquidity, investments and item processing) and forced a write-off of capital in natural person CU's (credit unions open to individuals versus institutions).

•Real estate values dropped 50% and more.

•Our CU had a high concentration (60% or more of total loans to members) in real estate and home equity loans.

•Delinquency increased in response to rising unemployment and the loss of home values.

•The regulatory climate was unpredictable; inconsistent; acrimonious and tyrannical.

•Provisions for loan and investment loss expenses increased to levels never seen.

•Operating expenses were not reduced fast enough in response to the signs, once known, and tough decisions were not made—actions like reducing the number of staff or closing branch locations.

•Traditional strategic planning models did not fit economic realities.

At a scenario planning session in the fall of 2007, I asked our executive leadership team, and the board of directors, to consider what assumptions did they feel were inviolate. Their answers were as follows:

1. Service matters and is more important than profit.
2. Take care of the employees, and they will take care of the members (customers).
3. Credit unions are different from banks.
4. Our credit union will always be here.
5. Our people matter and are the most important asset.

We knew that a sustainable, competitive advantage did not exist. Competition copies the success of others at a quick pace. The average company used to last about 50 years. Now it lasts about 25 years. And that will reduce to 10 years in the very near future. Our credit union was organized in 1953, and the national credit union movement began in 1908, with the Federal Credit Union Act coming in 1934.

Lack of innovation, along with the Great Recession and onerous, incompetent regulatory agencies were the causes of credit union numbers decreasing by one per day for several years.

Technology lags in the credit union movement, in part, because of the upfront costs. The bigger challenge is inertia, as in the lack of it, and management's "head in the sand" attitude. It goes something like this: "Hey, things are going great, do not screw with it. I'm getting merit raises, annual bonuses and the financial measurements are good. Why spend a million on a new core system?"

When a financial institution convenes to carry out strategic planning, it's under pressure from time constraints, attention spans and outside influences. Get it over by 4 pm on Friday—in time for dinner—and noon on Saturday—so we can keep tee times—and be darn sure the beer is cold and you have the correct vermouth for the Manhattans. Then, produce a paper trail that affirms something was accomplished.

Financial targets are often determined out of context. For example, if a board member has a personal agenda, that will determine how they interact with financial and non-financial metrics. Budgets often do not support the metrics or balanced scorecard.

There is rarely adequate time in the confines of a "weekend in the woods" to examine information and make informed decisions about where, when, who, costs, applicability to the organization and how to deliver products to members and potential members.

We identified what a killer competitor looked like under different scenarios. So how do organizations stand out as a killer competitor? By creating something that is very different. It would be well-capitalized, have strong management, know its members and have leading technology. We discussed what we had to do to survive across different scenarios identified as plausible and agreed that the characteristics of that killer competitor are the very ones we needed.

The critique of the planning session had nothing to do with the killer competitors we thought we'd figured out and prepared for. It was usually on how good the food, location and weather was.

Board members get to bring their spouses to a nice resort; all expenses paid, and in a casual setting, interact with each other and the executive leadership team. It is a good team building exercise and usually sets the direction for the next twelve months.

Said plans are rarely flexible enough, though, to withstand adversity. What can be counted on is that if the organization misses its milestones and targets, the regulatory agencies will roll up the plan and pop the CEO and board over the nose as you might do a puppy that wet the rug.

Regardless of how effective the plan is, adopting one is one of the fiduciary responsibilities board members must do. The objective is to provide its CEO with a clear understanding of the direction the board wants to see in the next twelve months and in the future. If the board agrees that management should be setting the priorities, then why meet annually to rehash the course the credit union has taken if reports indicate the course is producing satisfactory progress?

Long after the annual trip, the balanced scorecard (a strategic planning and management system used extensively in business and industry, government, and nonprofit organizations worldwide to align business activities to the vision and strategy of the organization, improve internal and external communications and monitor organization performance against strategic goals) still has to be revised to reflect reality, e.g.: rising delinquency, mortgage defaults, double-digit annual health insurance premium increases, slowing loan demand, inability to attract core deposits, etc.

In addition, our incentive plans were always tied to the balanced scorecard metrics, so we often 'needed' to make adjustments.

We regularly talked about being narrowly focused on measurements that mattered. Management was concentrating on increasing net worth and return on average assets (ROAA). Some of the balanced scorecard metrics were no longer relevant. For example, a director pushed their agenda of increasing the number of products per household by an unattainable number.

Our balanced scorecard became unbalanced. Hell, it came off its tracks. We were tracking ten or more metrics, many of which had no effect on income and profit. Not-for-profits must show a profit in order to continue. Call it excess revenues after operating expenses, or any name you want. Profits drive the engine and build capital, allowing the organization to provide products and services, and grow.

One can argue that we had taken a strategic direction that was not communicated by the balanced scorecard. The truth was that the current economic realities dictated a course correction was needed, and the scorecard wasn't flexible and contained metrics not appropriate to our needs. By measuring metrics that do not contribute to success or drive the economic engine, we increased operating expenses and put on the back burner the matters that required our attention. In any organization, what gets measured gets done. However, you can be doing the right things at the wrong time because you're not measuring the right things. Being busy is not taking right action. Right action is doing the right thing at the right time with the right people. How many times have you said to your boss how busy you are or had an employee or child tell you how busy they are as a way to deflect the fact that little progress toward the actual goal is getting done?

There are many members in credit unions who mistakenly believe, because someone else told them, that credit unions should always have the lowest loan rates and the highest CD rates. But, it's simply not true. You can go back to the origins of the cooperative movement, and there is no mention in any charter proclaiming the organization will always provide the lowest loan rates or highest savings rates. What you will find, is language that says, "...the organization was formed to provide access to credit at reasonable rates for prudent and provident purposes."

Many credit union members, who grew up during the Great Depression, passed that false tale onto their children. They feared the stock market and mutual funds, while their baby boomer children are apt to take their inheritance out of the credit union as quickly as they can after Mom and Dad die, investing it in index funds and other investment vehicles designed to throw off higher yields/income, with added risks.

Unlike banks, who raise capital by attracting deposits, credit unions have to do it the old-fashioned way...they earn it. Regulations on what is permissible for credit unions are more conservative than they are for banks. As deposits come into a credit union, they become a liability. That is, the member/depositor, is "loaning" the organization their money. The promise is that they will be paid a dividend and that the funds will be available for withdrawal upon demand. Here's the rub. The credit union uses that deposit to fund loan demand from other members. It looks like this: John Q. Member deposits $100 into a share account at his credit union. His credit union approves a request for an $85 loan from Mary B. Member at a rate that will both pay John the promised dividend, contribute to operating costs, and expected loan losses. The remaining $15 is invested. As long as Mary makes her loan payments, there are cash flows to provide liquidity if John requests a withdrawal and to approve more loans.

Having looked at other credit unions with growth and profits, we realized their plans were weighted towards maximizing profits and returning any excess profits above specified levels to the members. That could be in the form of lower loan rates, higher savings rates, more branches, a patronage dividend or some combination. Aggressively pursuing a narrow focus in itself pays off. The boards and management of those credit unions were focused and did not waiver in their mission, goals or objectives.

With the 4th quarter of 2007 drawing to an end, the budgeting process was in full swing. Our management team completed a major overhaul of the sales and service delivery systems to position the credit union for 2008 and beyond. The existing balanced scorecard metrics did not support our strategic direction. Be it the concept or implementation of the balanced scorecard, one thing was certain...it did not drive our plans. For example, the planning facilitator we employed for three years was a proponent that the volunteer board of directors must be involved in and determine the financial benchmarks. I did not agree.

We began to experience a tick up in loan defaults in late 2007; however, there were no red flags. ROAA decreased, but we had $14 million in reserves and were profitable. I had lived through several recessions, and we had a great strategic and scenario plan with a vision of growing assets to $500 million in seven years.

During an exit interview in late 2007, Mr. Jerk Wad, the NCUA supervisory examiner, said, "You are supposed to be smart people. How did you get into this mess?" Isn't that a gracious way to build rapport and open communication by calling your audience stupid? Those were his words at an exit interview with our board of directors, at which he embarrassed the subordinate female NCUA field examiner by ordering her to sit beside him so he could look at the examination report for the first time. We had never met him or even heard his name.

His female subordinate, herself a former credit union employee, did not tell us he was coming. Instead of coming into the meeting and spraying the room with testosterone, a respectful conversation may have uncovered the facts he wanted. He was more concerned that we should have met at a different restaurant than about the economy and its effect on our earnings.

We were not notified that he would attend so there was literally not enough seating in the small, circular room in the restaurant. It was an ambush. In hindsight, we should have declined the exit interview that evening and rescheduled it. The credit union's chair of the board later told me he felt like a caged animal at that meeting.

Jerk Wad was not prepared to meet with us and opened by saying he did not like driving to Sarasota from the east coast of the state where he lived in a deluxe, doublewide mobile home. In a display of exasperation, he blurted out that our salaries and benefits were the highest that he had ever seen.

Really? God bless the Internet. A simple search on NCUA's website (sorted by the 5300 reports for all credit unions in NCUA Region 3) showed more than two dozen examples that his statement was not true. Why would he make such an outrageous statement? Because there were no consequences for and oversight of his actions.

Leadership at NCUA has failed to establish an honor code. The appointed three-person board is political in nature. They serve six-year terms and POTUS appoints the chair, who is usually a member of the prevailing political party. They are up against entrenched federal employees and have no motivation or power to condemn unethical behavior.

Back in 2007, Joanne Johnson, a former NCUA Chair, at a meeting in Jacksonville hosted by VyStar CU, chided credit unions for not serving the under-served, not making small business loans and encouraged them to enter the home mortgage and indirect vehicle lending markets to serve their members. She said credit unions were sitting on too much capital and they should grow. If the arrogance of Jerk Wad and the comments of his boss appear inconsistent to you, I agree.

We hired an independent real estate loan expert, the same one that trained NCUA examiners, to consult and design our internal mortgage lending policies. We were not forced into real estate lending, but it was not a core competency. I never liked indirect vehicle lending, but we did it for a while. We got out of that when we held $11 million of indirect loans.

Indirect lending allows approved auto dealers, new and used, to enroll a person as a member in the credit union so the borrower(s) can take advantage of the lower loan rates offered. For the dealer's participation, the credit union pays a kick back of 1% of the amount financed, and offers the lowest rates possible to entice the dealer to refer business. That reduces the effective yield (earnings) on every loan.

The NCUA and Florida Office of Financial Regulation (OFR) examiners did not get the fact that our country was suffering and being shoved into economic turmoil, high unemployment, significant loss of real estate values, wars on different fronts that have been going on for years and the worst national deficit that any living person has seen. The country was in a five-year slide as revenues continued to disappoint and hiring freezes remained in effect.

U.S. Grant was correct when he said critics are generally those who know the least about the matter criticized.

Corporations and not-for-profits have a code of ethics, approved by their board of directors, that is usually published on their website and then hung in their employee lunchrooms and lobbies. The code of ethics is supposed to serve as a guide to officers and staff as well as convince stakeholders that they operate by the codes. What a code of ethics cannot do, however, is compel people to do the right thing, to be transparent and take personal responsibility.

Consider Rotary's Four-Way Test:

Of the things we think, say or do,

1. Is it the TRUTH?
2. Is it FAIR to all concerned?
3. Will it build GOODWILL and BETTER FRIENDSHIPS?
4. Will it be BENEFICIAL to all concerned?

Powerful guidelines, such as these, are in ethics codes around the globe. But what happens when most do not comply?

USA Today (08/08/11) ran an article in which the author claimed that 65% of workplace incivility is attributed to the leadership of the workplace and 59% may be attributed to the employees themselves. The article goes on to say workplace incivility is on the rise, e.g.; rudeness, insults and plain old bad manners. Research suggests that 75% to 80% of people have experienced incivility and it is a growing and prevalent problem. Some of the causes, according to the authors, are the economy, threats of layoffs and higher demands for increased productivity.

Let's take this a step further...

What happens when leadership allows workplace incivility...when honor, duty and trust are replaced by power and greed and the bad behavior they breed?

The Great Banking Collapse of 2008

# Chapter 3: Regulatory Purgatory

*"Mama always said: Life is like a box of chocolates. You never know what you're gonna get."*
--- Forrest Gump

Slate and federal regulators live in a protective bubble. Regardless of economic conditions, their lights come on every day. Often the regions in which they live are unaffected, as it was for the Atlanta, Georgia, and Washington, DC regulators, so, from their vantage point, they were oblivious.

Regulators have not, and will not, acknowledge that natural person credit unions (open to people) and corporate credit unions (open to credit unions) adhered to the laws, regulations and statutes, as evidenced by regular examinations. Credit unions and community banks, like the rest of our country, were harshly affected by the economic downturn as additional victims. They didn't cause it.

The strain of interacting with incompetent and bullish regulators and peers took a devastating toll on me. I have always had, and retain today, a deep-seated dislike for bullies, the people who prey on those weaker or in an inferior position in work or life, and those that believe they are immune to the consequences of their actions. That I have not been arrested for beating the snot out of more than a few of them is a testament to God's grace and larger plan for me.

The regulatory agencies, when times are good, typically examine a financial institution every 15-18 months. Each examination lasts three to five weeks and disrupts the entire organization and almost every employee in it. When economic conditions aren't good, such as during the Great Banking Recession, examiners show up unannounced and more frequently. They might begin showing up bi-weekly, stay for a week and then make a return trip, repeating the cycle.

It's a complete exercise in futility as the balance sheet and statement of operations changes are insignificant in such a short window of time. All financial and transactional data for most banks and credit unions are transmitted electronically monthly, or at most quarterly for smaller organizations. In fact, examination scrutiny can be almost entirely completed remotely using available technology. If technology were utilized to its full capabilities, examiners would not physically be on-site in any financial institution for 3 weeks or longer, return for an exit interview and then need up to 45 days to complete an examination report.

Each examination produces a report, and the financial institution must respond in writing. Examinations are a matter of written record, albeit not a public one. Our responses often ran eight or more pages and were reviewed by legal counsel in advance. Even when faced with irrefutable evidence that the examiner-in-charge (EIC) made a mistake, regulatory agencies did not correct the report of examination.

Anyone reading the exam has an incomplete picture of reality as many infractions are not technical violations of regulations or rules; and almost all of those are corrected during the examination process and are thus pointless to report. Additionally, the financial institution's response lays all that out.

Given the courtesy of correcting errors while the EIC is onsite, a lot of mistakes could be avoided. Regrettably, the examination report is frequently changed by leadership in the state capital or NCUA regional office. The EIC denies accountability and blames their bosses.

At an exit interview in early 2008, conducted at our Bee Ridge Road 2nd floor conference room, I had our board of directors, executive leadership team and Beetle Bailey (not his real name, and I apologize to Beetle Bailey for the unfavorable association), the state examiner who later became the area supervisory examiner and bears a striking resemblance to Warren Jeffs, the convicted cult leader, in attendance. Joining that meeting via telephone were our attorney and Olive Oil, (not her real name, and I apologize to Olive Oil for the unfavorable association), an NCUA special actions leader, and a director who called in from a restaurant.

Expecting a fight and having been burned already, I hired a court reporter to audio tape and provide a written transcript of that meeting. It was expected to be a contentious meeting, so I had asked and been assured that the two heads of the Florida OFR would attend in-person, or via telephone, and received assurances that they would. They did not attend as promised and no excuse was ever provided. I later learned that they were dining in Tallahassee at the time of the meeting.

The Warren Jeffs look alike and I were seated with our knees touching so we could be heard by those on the conference call. He admitted that he was powerless to challenge Tallahassee on the final report of examination and its contents. Even though he knew that most of the infractions were trivial and others had been corrected during then examination period and should not be in the final report.

The audio quality of that meeting was horrible. We had at least three persons joining via telephone, in different states, and the background noise made it difficult. Conversations cut out. The printed transcription was about as bad. I provided MP3 recordings to both the Florida OFR and NCUA. The NCUA examiner said it was the worst exit interview she had ever been a part of.

Though now retired, Captain Kangaroo (not his real name, and I also apologize to Captain Kangaroo for the unfavorable association), the area supervisory examiner, was at that time in poor health. In fact, he was morbidly obese, a heavy cigarette smoker, had suffered a stroke in one of his eyes so was thus unable to see, was diabetic and limped from a fall off a ladder at his home. He spent more time outside smoking and checking his blood sugar levels than he did supervising anything while openly counting the days to his retirement.

In prior periods, when financial conditions were almost optimal and the organization was running smoothly, he and I had an exit interview to discuss the CAMEL rating. That is a scale used by regulators on a scale of 1-5, with 1 being the highest. I asked what we had to do to earn a "1" in management. He said, "I could give you a 1 if that's what you want." I declined, with the explanation that there was no place to go but down from the highest perch and a good, solid "2" was fine with our board of directors, who are considered management for purposes of that rating system.

A disturbingly large portion of the examination grading system is subjective, versus objective. But even the objective system isn't logical. Objective items are graded within predetermined ranges established by the regulatory agencies. Those ranges are numerical and not always in the best interest of the organizations or their member-owners.

For example, to earn a "1" in the category of asset quality (the percentage of loans over 60 days in arrears), delinquency ratios need to be less than 1.25% and losses from charged off loans less than 0.25%. That is artificially low and leaves a lot on the table. To be that conservative, the organization must decline credit requests for too many members, and thus lose the interest income and late fees those loans would have provided. It flies in the face of the reason credit unions were organized, which is to provide credit at reasonable rates for prudent purposes.

We ran our organization with commonsense and for the members, and were able to keep a larger portion of the total savings deployed in loans to the owners. We maximized our income and not once in 20 years of examinations, did a regulator remark that our practices were unsound.

In predictable fashion, a team of examiners arrives midday Monday. Others arrive later that week or the next as needed, i.e.; specialists in the areas of lending, asset/liability management, investments and human resources. They spend the first week completing the work papers from the financial institution they spent the prior 3 weeks examining, completing their expense reports, etc. Not much gets done that first week. Go figure.

Sometimes the examiners needed assistance from members of our staff to locate a hotel in a safe area and one within the Florida OFR per diem policy. Such was the case for a team of female examiners from Dade County, Florida, who booked state approved per diem rooms in a hotel where the rooms are typically rented by the hour. Remember Jerk Wad, the NCUA supervisory examiner who questioned the cost of living in Sarasota? Sarasota was, and is, an expensive place to live. The state of Florida's per diem policy did not cover a hotel room in north Sarasota. Those women had to get an exception to per diem policy so we could help them find a safe place to stay that week.

On occasion, the examiners forgot to bring the 45 pounds of reports that were requested, copied and shipped to them, thereby requiring our staff to waste time and money copying and producing the same information a second time. They all leave at midday on Friday, and the process repeats itself each week. Often, I observed an examiner playing solitaire on his government issued laptop.

In years prior to the collapse, the examiners would arrive early, introduce themselves to the CEO, and ask to be escorted to a meeting room. They would identify each member of their team, leave a business card with the receptionist so calls could be forwarded to the meeting room and then introduce themselves to the members of the executive team.

By late 2007, they would come in, go directly to the meeting room and speak to nobody unless spoken to. Civility had been abandoned, and they always had something negative to say. I literally did not know they were in our building at times, until I spotted them and spoke first.

We always asked the examiners to sit down and meet with me and the executive leadership team and receive a verbal report of current plans and issues. I always asked to be notified at the end of each day of material findings or violations or the lack thereof. I did not want, or expect, to be surprised later.

Examiners review internal controls, policies, compliance with laws and regulations and state statutes. They are not decision-makers and have virtually no practical or contemporary experience in the industry they are regulating. The examiners often voice their personal opinions, but do not do so in writing.

That isn't their job, or their privilege. If they cannot find an obvious violation, they have been known to cite an obscure or recently circulated regulation that the financial institution may not know about. But forget having a reasonable dialogue about the new regulations. Interestingly enough, they usually lost their ability to speak if a recording was made of the conversations or if our legal counsel was present.

We had a "throw them a bone" practice, meaning simple infractions, i.e.; missing paystubs in loan files, a misfiled document, or action that had little consequence, kept the examiners from looking further. The examiner-in-charge needs fodder for the report and will intuitively stop looking when they feel they have sufficient information with which to submit a report of examination. It is as if changing a wet baby gets it to stop crying. Throw them a bone gets them to stop looking.

In the absence of a technical violation of rules, statutes, or a board approved policy, the financial institution continues business as usual for the next 15-18 months until the examiners return.

The examination teams are almost always the same personnel. They rotate the examiner-in-charge title amongst them to satisfy an internal control requirement. In practice, the area supervisor is there and dominates the examination and exit interview. Think of your job. If your supervisor sat there and judged every word or corrected you in front of your clients, how would that make you feel?

The examination process is ineffective and adds little value, an opinion I voiced with NCUA and for which I was rebuked. Examinations and audits stare backward at financial results reflecting decisions made under different interest rate environments and assumptions.

Ever watched a cat trying to cover up a turd on a ceramic tile floor? That cat is busy as all get out. Nothing productive is getting accomplished. And there you have it! The best metaphor I can conjure up for the ineffectiveness of both federal and state examiners.

The examination process, apart from the inclusion of laptops and spreadsheets, is as antiquated as green visors, sleeve protectors and #2 pencils. Some examiners still count cash in teller drawers. What if by chance the examiner found that cash was $5 short? It isn't material and poses no significant risk. It does waste a half-hour for the examiner and the teller.

We, like many, had placed all loan files and the general ledger on a mainframe computer, requiring them to use a computer instead of paper. The examiners hated that and wanted the paper files. But, they got used to it.

Another example of the ineffectiveness of the examination process in Florida is the request for a biography of each elected official and officer every time they plan an examination. Florida statutes require all elected directors, committee members and officers to file an extensive background document within 30-days of their election or appointment. That Report of Officials is filed with the Florida Office of Financial Regulation (FLORIDA OFR), Division of Financial Institutions Tallahassee. FLORIDA OFR is the repository of those forms, yet the field examiners do not have them and repeatedly request the credit unions to get them new copies. We made a photocopy of the original filings and gave that to the examiners each visit, stale dated as it was, and they never questioned it.

When asked why they request information for which they are the repository, I was told they need to know their audience at exit interviews. My board thought that absurd and wondered why the credit union was not provided the qualifications of the examiners.

Legal counsel confirmed that there is no statute that compels compliance, unless the organization is under a Letter of Understanding and Agreement (LUA). Not to do so; however, just pisses them off and the retaliation isn't worth it. Note: LUA's were issued like candy by NCUA beginning in 2008. So much so, that there was no clout behind a LUA and our attorney and the NCUA examiner said so.

Examiners are concerned with form over substance. Provide a preponderance of paper, lots of 3-ring binders, and they salivate. Bring out a tape recorder and/or your attorney at an exit interview and the examiners become speechless. The first time we recorded an exit interview, and asked legal counsel to be present, was the result of a FLORIDA OFR examiner from Lakeland, Florida, near retirement, bringing our newly hired CFO to tears over his opinion of an assumed infraction of an internal policy.

In our board's approved policies, spouses and guests may be invited to meal functions. The FLORIDA OFR examiner told our CFO that she could go to jail because her fiancée shared dinner with the board and other guests at a planning session. The examiner was unwilling to admit a simple mistake or that state statutes are moot on guests at meal functions and the amount paid for the meals were insignificant.

With legal counsel operating a tape recorder and asking him questions, he was embarrassed and defensive in front of his boss, the NCUA team, and our board of directors. It was a senseless and foolish error in judgment on his part.

FLORIDA OFR staff earns less than their federal NCUA counter-parts and are subservient to NCUA when both are involved on the same examination. FLORIDA OFR's statutes parallel those of NCUA, and on almost all matters, FLORIDA OFR defers to or notifies NCUA on requests from state-chartered, federally-insured credit unions.

The FLORIDA OFR rarely denies any by-laws amendment. Florida credit unions know it is expeditious to be a state-chartered organization. The reason being is Florida-chartered versus federally-chartered credit unions know they have more flexibility and are rarely denied any by-laws amendment, i.e.; expansion of field of membership.

Almost every credit union in Florida has a community charter that allows them to serve persons living or working in any county they choose. Some federally-chartered credit unions converted to a state-charter for that reason. The FLORIDA OFR was managed by an entrenched-staff who had been there too long and were out of touch.

What purpose does Florida OFR serve? It is an advantage, to a point, for a financial institution to be chartered under the state. Were that not so, one of the largest credit unions in Florida would not have switched their charter from a federal one. NCUA is the 800-pound gorilla and FLORIDA OFR is deferential to it. It could be an expense reduction to Florida's taxpayers to abolish the FLORIDA OFR. Both NCUA and Florida OFR are overly invasive, over-funded and underperforming.

For example, when the letter of intent to merge was executed between me and the surviving credit union CEO, Fred Flintstone, Chief of Credit Union Regulation (not his real name, and I apologize to Fred Flintstone for the unfavorable association) told me that FLORIDA OFR's only concern was that the surviving organization remain state-chartered so FLORIDA OFR's revenues weren't affected. Examination fees are based upon a combination of assets, income and in some case the number of members a credit union has.

I said earlier, the state and federal regulatory agencies do not give a shit about the organization or its people. It is about preserving their revenue and the insurance fund.

An interesting side note is that the FLORIDA OFR examiners are prohibited from accepting the courtesy of a bottle of water or cup of coffee. NCUA examiners are not. Odd being as they all sit in the same room while onsite, and it creates resentment that one group is permitted to accept a common courtesy from the financial institution, the other is not.

Are the ethics of the state examiners so fragile that a cup of coffee may influence their report?

They were worried about bottles of water and complimentary coffee but ignorant when it came to the real issues causing all of us to lose.

There is a disturbing pattern that even though this great country (and I have literally placed my life at-risk to defend our rights) was founded upon the concept of free speech, regulatory examiners, and their leaders, feel that free speech is their right and does not apply to others.

Case in point, during one of several interminably long and meandering diatribes, I said to Beetle Bailey, the pontificating FLORIDA OFR area supervisor, that I was a reasonable person. There were some in other credit union's that may not be and that the stress of the challenges we were all facing could push some over the edge and that he might consider his tone and actions in that light. He said, "...while FLORIDA OFR employees are not protected, NCUA's employees are, and you better watch your choice of words."

When someone is threatening your career and ability to provide for your family, tensions are likely to rise and it is common sense not to fan the flames. One of my friends, and another credit union CEO, living and working in Ft. Meyers, went home one night and swallowed a bullet while his wife and child were in the other room. Seemingly, because of an encounter with a micromanaging, unsupportive board and examiners who together posed a direct threat to his ability to provide for his family.

Humans are emotive and can only be pushed so far before there's a reaction. The mildest person among us will still protect our family when threatened. I had a long conversation about the time of my own setbacks with a friend in Tampa who was a Credit Union CEO, a Vietnam vet and was dealing with the same state and federal examiners I was. He said he was also close to exploding as Olive Oil and Betty Rubble (not her real name, and I apologize to Betty Rubble for the unfavorable association), were threatening his livelihood, as they had done to me, by suggesting that he give up and merge into another credit union.

Point of clarification here...that is not their job. That fiduciary responsibility resides with the duly elected board of directors of the credit union.

Thankfully, it never happened. He made it through. And so did I. I'm relieved, but surprised, that due to the hundreds of organizations wiped out by the Great Banking Collapse of 2008 and the horrendous behavior of state and federal examiners, it didn't cause violence.

In the largest corporate credit union(s), a NCUA specialist trained in asset liability rules and investments was stationed in-house and sat in on committee meetings. The NCUA would later discipline their own employees, seize control of the organizations and sell assets at huge losses.

NCUA then required natural person credit unions to pay unprecedented assessments to recover the loss to the share insurance fund caused by their actions. Management and the boards of directors at these corporate credit unions were removed and sued by NCUA.

Those professionals did only what NCUA permitted in its regulations and did so under constant supervision and scrutiny by the NCUA. There was litigation on that subject, and former executives of a $345 billion corporate credit union seized by NCUA allege that NCUA itself put the corporate credit union out of business.

This is why I'm convinced more than ever that most of us in the industry didn't fail. We were forced and tricked into losing.

Regulators are one-trick ponies. They believe the only way to reverse an economic downturn is to slash operating expenses. It doesn't occur to them that increasing revenues, in addition to prudent expense controls, could be a more productive path. Once a business loses its ability to control its income streams, it is effectively out of business. That is what happened to us.

NCUA and FLORIDA OFR have been the root cause of the failure of hundreds of financial organizations because they disapproved of conservative capital restoration plans submitted by the financial institutions to increase revenue and reduce expenses. Focusing on "do not's" and framing everything in negative phrases or regulations is not sustainable.

Regulatory agencies are not inherently bad, they just have ineffectual leadership. People want to be led by persons with honor and integrity. People crave structure and accountability. The appointed leadership of our regulatory agencies change with each election result, and senior leadership positions are held most often by persons with no leadership experience or training. They are political appointees to whom favors are owed.

Given the economic misery of the times, the majority of financial institutions reduced staff, cut salaries, halted or reduced contributions to retirement plans and cut operating expenses. As credit union executives, we lived this misery, but our leadership at the NCUA made decisions as if they operated on a different planet.

For example, they increased staff levels, approved pay increases, and spent millions on travel. During that same time frame, credit unions were laying off staff, reducing pay, cancelled all travel and suspended contributions to 401-k plans.

On November 29, 2010, the CU Times reported, "The budget approved for NCUA for 2011 includes a 6.1% pay raise for employees covered by the collective bargaining agreement. That covers 80% of the agency's employees, and that three-year contract is up for renegotiation next year. The remaining 20% of employees are slated to receive a 3% increase, which was approved by the NCUA Board. The $225.4 million 2011 budget funds 1,209 full-time equivalent employees. It's a 12% increase over this year's budget of $200.9 million, which funds 1,130 FTEs."

The CU Times also reported, "NCUA Chairperson Debbie Matz said while credit unions are making progress, the agency is well aware of the "stressed financial environment" facing many credit unions, and that is why the agency is increasing the size of its examination staff and making the examination process more rigorous. The 2011 budget approved by the NCUA Board includes funds to add 78 people to the examination staff, including 60 field staff."

As the number of federally insured credit unions continued to decline from a high of 22,000 to the current 5,966 (September 2016) on the way to an expected 5,000, the additional field staff is counter-intuitive. The rate they're going, credit unions may soon have a one-to-one representative at the NCUA.

As another example, in March 2010, the Credit Union National Association (CUNA) reported that NCUA reiterates "the importance of effective liquidity risk management for the safety and soundness of financial institutions." Liquidity is cash flow. All businesses must have positive cash flows. This statement was issued at a time when credit unions were flush with deposits as members continued a flight to safety and withdrew from the stock market and banks. Credit union loan-to-share (deposit) ratios reduced as people were timid about taking on debt, and regulators had placed undue restrictions on lending.

The statement in March 2010 by NCUA is untruthful at best in as much as liquidity concerns did not exist, and any risk of liquidity in the credit union system was caused in part by NCUA's capricious takeover of US Central and WESCORP. By 2010, the great recession had been pronounced as over. Credit policies were still tight, and I know of no credit union in 2010 that experienced any challenges meeting daily cash flow requirements. As banks continued to shoot themselves in the foot with fees, credit unions gained market share and cash.

A Dade County Florida NCUA Capital Markets Specialist told me a 20% cash ratio (1/5 of assets) was a minimum; however, there is no regulation as to any percentage. That was his personal opinion, and unchecked by his superiors, he no doubt continues to espouse it to others. The damage that comes from financial institutions enacting policy based upon an examiner's personal opinion can be significant.

At best, it creates confusion as the next examiner will come in and say, "Why did you do this?" Then they will express their opinion, also not one based on rule or regulation, and the financial institution changes the policy again. We did that in response to an investment policy that a NCUA examiner said he didn't understand. We made the changes to appease him, and sure enough, he came back in

18 months and didn't recall the conversation or understand the policy that was revised at his request. The most contentious disagreement I had with FLORIDA OFR was over liquidity. Our CFO, who was also a CPA, prepared an in-depth study of daily cash inflows and outflows over a 2 year period and created an excel spreadsheet because examiners love a spreadsheet. That sheet demonstrated that at no point in the past two years had the organization needed more than $11.0 million in cash or its equivalents for daily operations.

The examiners wanted a policy that said 20% of assets, and it really pissed them off that the facts disproved their opinion. No regulation existed at that time to support their line of reasoning. The analysis verified $11.0 million each business day was well thought-out and that happened to be 5% of assets based on assets of $235.0 million.

We believed that holding $47 million in cash (20% of $235 million) in a non-earning asset to be detrimental to earnings. Working with a former NCUA official, the liquidity policy was revised and approved by our autonomous board of directors. It read, "liquidity shall be 5% of assets, or a sum certain as determined by the analysis."

Had I spit in the face of Fred Flintstone, the chief of credit union regulation, the impact would have been no different. He wanted 20%; but had no authority to do so. What followed was months of angry exchanges, childlike temper tantrums, and as the FLORIDA OFR took away our ability to control our revenues and expenses. They got their way.

For an example, Fred Flintstone forbid us to continue an auto loan recapture program that assisted our members in reducing the rate of interest on auto loans originated elsewhere. He forbid us to grant small business loans. He forbid us to manage our business out of the Great Recession.

It was a major cause of the merger. It was also a matter of principle I should not have fought. I never had a chance in an unfair fight and had to tie one-half of my brain behind my back so we could communicate at the same level. What we have in this country is an Imperial Regulatory. Add a crown and a robe and it would be complete. Bureaucrats know everything, just ask them. They believe they are more knowledgeable than the professionals and the boards of directors of financial institutions, and believe they know the membership and community's needs, despite not living or working there, or ever having worked in a financial institution.

Administrators in charge of the regulatory agencies make decisions that are not always based on fact or law. Every day, another credit union is slapped with a Letter of Understanding and Agreement (LUA) or a Document of Resolution (DOR) by NCUA. As aforementioned, LUA's are a nuisance and carry no weight. A DOR, on the other hand, is the way that NCUA begins to create a war chest so when they deny your net worth restoration plans, or force you to merge out of existence. They have covered their asses.

Often, NCUA refuses to provide the regulation, or rule, upon which they are penalizing the organization. They have also been known to deny a request under the Freedom of Information Act, to release a copy of a LUA. There is an overwhelming amount of evidence and stories about the abusive actions of state and federal regulatory agencies. Where there is this much smoke, it is highly probable that there's fire.

*See Appendix A for a list of grievances signed by numerous Credit Union CEOs.*

It may be as far-fetched to expect an examiner that has been in the state or federal system for any length of time to possess the skills or knowledge to look through a positive lens as it is to expect that politicians will suddenly become honest and cooperative with the other party and their constituents.

I referenced DFCS earlier when I shared the story of trying to help my little brother. When I think of inefficient and poorly lead organizations, they are on the top of my mind. Like the state and federal regulatory agencies, appointed leadership changes often, and has no stake in the successful implementation of a culture, honor code or accountability. When a child dies in foster care, you read about the failures of DFCS. You don't read about FLORIDA OFR or NCUA being responsible for the demise of a credit union or the undoing of careers and lives.

By 2008, I was far, far away from honor and duty; instead, I was neck deep in corporate scandal, embezzlement, massive monetary loses, and greed, hallmarks of Wall Street and big banks.

# Chapter 4: The Bane of Management is Micro-Managing

*"The person who says it cannot be done should not interrupt the person who is doing it."*
--- Chinese Proverb

O ur credit union was organized in December 1953 with the school board as the original sponsor, and it served all persons living or working in a three county area along Florida's Gulf Coast. The organization merged into it employees of the Sheriff's Department, all County employees, the newspaper, Venice Hospital and Loral Data Systems. The management team was experienced, stable and professional.

The organization actively planned for its future using outside resources and a balanced scorecard. The board of directors was comprised of seven volunteers, which experienced turnover without term limits. Three directors had 30+ years of experience, others had 10+ years and just one had less than one-year of experience.

This was a quality board of directors who did a lot of thinking about who served. The chair did not serve more than two years. The board had job descriptions and an orientation procedure. Governance was discussed often and a governance policy was approved to maintain consistency.

*See Appendix B for additional information on the organization.*

That last point is highly relevant as examinations of our credit union, independent CPA audits and internal audits never observed policies or practices that were unsafe. In the end, Olive Oil, the NCUA problem case officer, wrote in a letter to our board of directors, "...this is an economic event and not a management incident." From a NCUA examiner, that is approaching praise. She affirmed that we did nothing wrong.

The top issues that dominated the financial services industry in 2007 were the economy and the decline in home values and increase of unemployment levels. Florida and the other Sand States were severely affected. As a result of the loss of jobs, there were dramatic increases in loan defaults. The seizure of the corporate credit unions by NCUA and the impact to already stressed credit union balance sheets, and income statements, added fuel to the flames.

The same NCUA problem case officer who wrote, "...this is an economic event and not a management incident," blurted out in front of my executive leadership team that we should just go ahead and merge. I responded that that was a conversation best had in private, and it was also premature. She had played her hand in 2008 and was basically notifying us of NCUA's intent. At NCUA headquarters, word went out throughout the nation to merge and exterminate as many problem credit unions as possible, and to do so quickly.

I told the board of directors that things were bad and would get worse. I said if they would stay and fight, I would not leave them. I had been recruited over the years for larger organizations and had even gone on a few interviews. The board knew that and had been generous with compensation, retirement and an employment agreement.

The State & NCUA examiners were not helpful in any way and provided no assistance in the preparation of a net worth restoration plan. Brad Anderson, one of our directors, wrote to me, "I still feel we could have hung on and survived with the assistance of some decent regulators, examiners, etc."

Did the regulatory agencies cause the economic crises? No. Did they provide any assistance, an infusion of capital, or TARP funds like the banks received for the bailouts? Absolutely none.

The NCUA and the FLORIDA OFR buried their heads in the sand and prayed that the mess would go away. In doing so, they were complicit in more than 1100 credit unions going out of business. That equates to thousands of people losing their income and the ability to provide for their families. As I previously stated, almost none were ever able to secure another job that was comparable in wages and benefits.

If that claim sounds a little hard to believe, consider that there were 8,332 credit unions in the U.S. in 2008. By 2012, there were 7,165. That reduction continues at a rate of about 20 mergers per month! The big are getting bigger, while the number of small credit unions (with less than $50 million in assets) are shrinking. If current trends hold, in the next 20 years, half the credit unions around today will be gone.

It's an alarming trend, and here's why...

Credit unions help regulate loan and deposit rates for all Americans, not just their members. Bank customers benefit from the competition, although banks control about 93% of all consumer deposits in America. The shrinkage in the number of credit unions closely matches what we have seen in Canada and Australia, where the number of autonomous credit unions has been shrinking for decades. I expressed the view, but it warrants repeating here. Fewer credit unions should be a contributing factor for reducing the number of federal and state examiners; however, that is not happening.

20/20 hindsight being what it is, I think our credit union could have survived. I failed to check my ego and argued with the NCUA and FLORIDA OFR when that was counter-productive. Our CFO did not feel we could have survived. Our CPA firm, who had managed 40+ mergers, believed that we could have survived with further cuts to staffing and an additional $1.0 million in expense reductions. Our fourth rendition of a net worth restoration plan predicted net worth may sink to 3.5% and that we would need three years to get back to 7%.

Alonzo Swann, the NCUA Regional Director, disapproved the plan without comment or alternative suggestions. There were other credit unions in Florida, and the other Sand States, with worse numbers that were allowed to continue.

At the time, I believed merger was the only option. With the benefit of several years to reflect, however, I wish we had revised the net worth plan and plugged in numbers that told a different story. Yes, the economic situation was volatile and fraught with uncertainty. Yes, interest rates, defaults, unemployment, expenses and income all affected the profit and loss statements. But I think we had a shot…a long one, but a shot none-the-less.

Could we have reduced staff by another 11 positions (we had already dropped from 80 to 63 full-time employees), implemented an additional $1.0 million in revenue per year and reduced assets to raise the net worth ratio? Yes. There is nobody at NCUA or FLORIDA OFR who could have proven or disproven whatever forecast we put forth.

It is worth telling that Olive Oil, the NCUA problem case officer, took our restoration plan and ran it through an Excel spreadsheet of her own design. In her pro forma, it indicated that a 1% assessment of our assets that NCUA had commanded to cover losses to its share insurance fund from all credit unions was forecast to continue into infinity.

I questioned her assumption and asked if she knew something that nobody else did? Adding, or omitting, an annual assessment of $2.3 million dollars (1% of total assets) was life or death to our organization. Her assumption that the 1% annual assessments were to continue was flawed and above her pay grade. Her response was, "It's just a spreadsheet, I cannot change it, so don't worry about it."

Again, this was a mandate upon all credit unions, not just ours. The consequences weighed heavily in determining cash flows and profits, even though the NCUA kept a separate set of books illustrating profits and losses with, and without, the assessments.

Her little spreadsheet was so much more than "It's just a spreadsheet."

The flawed data was used, in part or in its entirety, by Alonso Swann, the grand poohbah in Atlanta at that time, to reject our net worth restoration plan. The assessments were reduced a few more times and ended entirely within 18 months. There was nothing we could do to overcome an additional $2.3 million per year of operating expenses. Remember: our net worth restoration plan illustrated that we could increase revenues by $1.0 million per year via staff reductions and increasing profits.

This is the why, along with the liquidity argument of keeping 20% of assets in cash, I threw in the towel. We were denied the ability to fight the good fight and summarily forced to commit suicide. We lost. We didn't fail.

In the end, I made a decision that affected 63 employees, 27,000 members and the landscape in Sarasota, Florida's financial institutions for eternity. That choice was made under great duress and with conflicting opinions from those around me.

I was influenced in my thoughts and actions by the threat of personal loss should NCUA and FLORIDA OFR force a merger or issue a cease and desist order, which would effectively make null and void my employment agreement and supplemental retirement plan.

In October 2009, when the merger took effect, I was 59 years old. The country was in its deepest economic trough in 80 years. I was scared and angry. I regret allowing that to cloud my thinking. But, the times were stressful and my emotions were high…and I was controlled by fear.

Had the NCUA slapped a cease and desist order on the organization, they would be empowered to remove me, nullify all employment agreements, supplemental retirement plans, remove the board of directors, cancel contracts and agreements with vendors, etc. I believed, and that was proven to be the case, that I would not be able to find a similar position in that economy, and all the protections afforded me in the employment and retirement agreements would be null and void. The financial impact would have been devastating and irreparable.

Credit Union philosophy is deeply imbedded in me. It was in our organization, too. And, that used to be so for all credit unions. Today, philosophy is no longer considered good business. As a Credit Union Development Educator, I have spoken to audiences on the virtues of keeping mission and philosophy in the forefront.

Leaders in credit unions today are recruited from banks and accounting backgrounds, as are volunteer directors, so they lack an appreciation of our roots. The NCUA and FLORIDA OFR never cared about credit union history and philosophy at all.

The kind of stress their leadership, or lack thereof, has caused was and is self-inflicted. Focusing on numbers only, and not the employees and members, is a mistake. In a movement that was founded upon the philosophy of service, it cannot be successful simply by cutting expenses and service.

# Chapter 5: Get Back to Basics

*"This is a football."* ---Vince Lombardi

To survive, we had to get back to basics. Serve the members. Have fun and make money. If your employees are happy, your earnings increase. Are you having fun? Is your organization having fun? Do you enjoy your work? Answer in the affirmative, and you're a survivor.

But here's the climate we operated in, as posted to many blogs supporting those of us in banking and credit unions who were dealing with the stress and emotions of the Great Collapse:

*"While mergers may be listed as 'voluntary', very, very few of them are. Having been an NCUA examiner, I have been sent to a CU and TOLD to merge it. (These are always, 'voluntary.' Even if NCUA requires it.) Regardless of whether or not it was sustainable. This is simply NCUA's preferred method of dealing with small problems they consider not worth their time. Too bad, most could have been saved with little or no cost, and not been gobbled up just to make a minor addition to a megalithic credit union."* --- B.W., August 18, 2009.

*"Researchers only reviewed crime scene. A true CSI team would have interviewed witnesses. Please do follow up and talk to managers and boards of target CU's. I think you will find that many mergers were result of retirement of a long-time manager and a board that was pressured by regulators and sweet talked by acquirer CU's. Also, look the capital ratio of the target CU's to see how "unhealthy" they really were. Small CU's must be preserved. They are not only our poster child of the image we want to project but they are on the front line helping each member by lending on basis of character instead of score. Some "mega" CU's could have learned from them."* --- T.C., August 21, 2009

*"We are a small credit union that is being pushed into a merger before the net worth restoration plan can be voted up or down. We are holding out for NCUA to be the bad person and are trying to enlist our government officials to look into this trend. I believe it is no more than a way for NCUA of thinning the herd so they don't have us little credit unions to "deal" with. Once the herd is thinned then the taxing can begin. Remember although NCUA thumps their chest that they are here to "regulate" the credit unions they are still a government entity. By the government and for the government and the government is running out of choices on who to tax. Certainly it will not be the big credit unions with an exemption for the small credit unions. Therefore, get rid of the small people and viola no more worries. EVERYBODY gets taxed. By the way, I saw the subprime lending crash coming months before it happened. I have an insight for disaster and its heading towards taxation of credit unions."* --- G.D., August 18, 2009

*"I know what you mean about Credit Unions...they sure have changed in the past couple of years – a lot harder to*

*make a buck with NCUA taking it away from you as soon as you make it. "I retired in 2005 and am so glad that I did. I think I got out at just the right time…before things in our nation and in credit unions began to turn so sour."* --- A 35 + year industry veteran.

*"Interesting thing, I am on the Federal Reserve committee, as you know, and the banks controlled by the FDIC are crying far louder than we are. You should hear some of the horror stories they tell. Actually made me feel a little better. There is a coming realization by the Fed that all the regulations and stiff examinations are slowing loan growth and costing way too much. We'll see if that goes anywhere."* --- A 35 + year industry veteran.

*"I wish that I had a positive story to share about examiners/regulators this past couple of years but it isn't possible. I personally believe they have been the "tidal wave" of destruction in our industry because of their lack of understanding and willingness to give credit unions the latitude to serve their members in these difficult times. If not for my job and my career I would have reacted strongly to them but they were the "Gods" and we had little if any recourse. I felt even the trade associations abandoned us during those times. I am sharing this with you confidentially and do not wish for my name to be used. As much as I hate to admit it, I still fear the repercussions that could develop if we openly speak out about these situations. One comment, which says it all to me, was from Larry Peters, a FLORIDA OFR supervisor. I quote "In my opinion if your members cannot afford to pay their mortgage payments then you need to tell them to call Mayflower and start packing their boxes" end quote. It was Larry who said it, but Robert Hayes, chief of credit union regulation knew about it. I will never forget*

*that comment because it proved to me the complete lack of understanding on the part of the regulators. They had secure jobs and nothing to worry about so the only answer was something ridiculous like that. I literally almost had a stroke that day when he said that to me. Again, I ask that it be kept as a confidential comment. You are free to say it is from a 30+ year credit union executive but nothing that would identify me. This saddens me but I have to be realistic."* --- 30+ Year Credit Union Executive

# Chapter 6: Accountability and Clarity

*"The supreme quality for leadership is unquestionably integrity. Without it, no real success is possible, no matter whether it is on a section gang, a football field, in an army, or in an office."* --- Dwight D. Eisenhower

Why are the country, and you and I, having this conversation about leadership?

News agencies report spectacular leadership failures. We see the dysfunction in Washington, DC, and often, in our state and local offices, school boards, etc. So many people in leadership positions are incompetent, and, in many cases, dishonest.

What happened to honor, humility, respect and service?

Today, our country is crying for positive leadership and a value system.

Bad leadership does offer a learning opportunity as these faulty leaders teach us why leaders fail; what they do or don't do to negatively influence a situation. Good leaders are those who are willing to study these failures, listen to the opinions of others on all sides, make positive changes and then be accountable for the results the changes bring.

Leaders, too, need quality supervision. It was reported, for example, that David Sokol, a senior executive and heir-apparent to Warren Buffet, might have violated a conflict of interest statement. Mr. Buffet gathered information and concluded there had been a violation, and Mr. Sokol resigned.

I make no judgment as to the seriousness of the alleged ethical transgressions; however, the lesson is that there were consequences for his actions and they were enforced.

Another example of bad leadership can be found in the airline industry. Consumers are unsatisfied with the airlines and complaints are at all-time highs. Why? There are many reasons, but one that leaps out is a lack of accountability and clarity. There is no accountability for flights being delayed or cancelled; flights being overbooked, lost luggage; a pricing system that defies understanding; and no senior executive is ever available to speak to a consumer that has a complaint or to clarify policies that have dismal results.

I answered my own phone and had no administrative assistant to screen calls and act as my gatekeeper, which, by the way, is not true in most banks and credit unions, or for that matter, in most organizations. Personal accountability has been delegated and clarity of mission and purpose all but forgotten. We've lost our community of manners and supplanted that with a sense of self-importance and excessive, greed-driven ambition.

It is important to know your craft or trade and to honor your audience/customer/client. Simply defending your position does not create better oversight. Leaders and regulators are not entitled to make up facts that serve their interests, and their interests only.

Clarity and truth can be achieved when all participants understand and respect that there are rewards and consequences for every action.

Integrity does matter. In a study by Robert Half Management Resources, it was concluded that beyond technical and functional expertise, the following traits were high on an organization's list of leadership requirements.

(The survey included 1,400 CFO's from a random sample of U.S. companies with 20 or more employees (December 2010)). The results were:

•Integrity-33%
•Interpersonal/Communication Skills-28%
•Initiative-15%
•Ability to Motivate Others-12%
•Business Savvy-10%

The Great Banking Collapse of 2008 was proof that integrity was lost. In the financial services and banking industries, we are not investing the time and resources to instill a culture of values, integrity, or taking right actions for the right reasons. That lack of institutional integrity has been documented as a cause for many corporations and organizations going out of business, suffering from massive public embarrassment and extreme financial losses. It's now documented as a cause of the 2008 Banking Collapse.

In the state of Georgia, my adopted home, funding was cancelled for the Department of Ethics. The State of Florida has a Commission on Ethics, with a statement on its website that Florida has been a leader among states in establishing ethics standards for public officials. Apparently, that department was on vacation in 2008.

You cannot lead others unless you lead yourself. The regulatory agencies set themselves up as disciplinarians. But, if they are so disciplined, why don't they discipline themselves to lead from the front and tell the truth? There is no leadership guiding the regulatory employees through any process of accountability or responsibility.

If a team of competent, honorable employees were all pulling in the same direction, they could be a formidable force for good. Most people do not accept accountability without a nudge. They are lead to accountability. They have to be shown what's in it for them, how it helps them grow professionally and personally and ensures the future of their agency and their place in it, and thus supports their livelihood.

The NCUA and FLORIDA OFR examiners work in small teams, far removed from their respective headquarters. They are isolated, almost universally disliked, complain about being underpaid and are away from their families for weeks on end. They can, and do, say improper things and inject personal opinions into financial institution operations, without any basis in the rule and regulations they're supposed to be operating by.

In 29 years in credit unions, except in the case mentioned below, I never received an acknowledgement that an examiner's or field supervisor's actions, deeds, or words were inaccurate or false, or that a report of examination contained erroneous information that could have been corrected while the examiners were on-site.

The one exception I mentioned above was in reference to the FLORIDA OFR area supervisor, the one who looks like Warren Jeffs. He had complained to me that his salary was less than that of a schoolteacher. His bureau chief said to me that his employee's comments were not appropriate. Of course, the area supervisor never apologized and wasn't disciplined or held accountable, to my knowledge.

He began his career in 1989 and, at the time (2009), was earning $73, 413. I may not be the brightest bulb in the box, but I do know that is more than an average schoolteacher is paid. Public employees' salaries may be verified on the Internet. Why would he misrepresent that? Pettiness. Low morale. And there were no consequences for his actions.

The average salary at the time he made that absurd comparison paid to a Florida public K-12 school teacher for the 2009-10 school year was $46,696, which was a decrease of $242 (-0.52 percent) over the average salary of $46,938 for the 2008-09 school year. Teachers are underpaid and entrusted with our greatest resources—our children. They don't deserve the unfavorable comparison to an examiner entrusted with nothing except his or her ego.

Fred Flintstone, Chief, Bureau of Credit Union Regulation, was an interesting person. I believe he's now retired. He's a former banker, small town mayor and by all accounts a nice person. In researching this book, I looked on the State's website and saw that he began with the State of Florida in 1967. I thought that odd in as much as I had been told of his banking and political career. So, I called and spoke with him and said I was working on a book, and I asked about the dates of his employment.

He laughed and said as a 17-year old he worked one summer in Chattahoochee at the hospital. He had a long career doing other things and had been hired by FLORIDA OFR just a few years prior. I asked if he was excusing the incorrect facts represented on the state's website that imply he is the longest serving state employee, perhaps ever. He said it was kind of cool but admitted it was incorrect. He said he hoped to read my book when it was completed. Pony up your money, Fred, and you can.

It's no wonder FLORIDA OFR's Area Supervisor acted in dishonorable ways. The chief above him does the same. And when the supervisors aren't ethical, honorable and accountable, it leads to field staffs of the same mold.

The field staffs of FLORIDA OFR, and those of NCUA, too, are discontented. Most of them could have increased their income by going into the private sector. NCUA examiners earn up to $140,000, which is more than many of the CEO's in small credit unions. Some could be CFOs in a credit union or bank, or an accountant, internal auditor, etc.

They would travel less and be with their families more. Why do they persist in remaining in unsatisfying jobs and then complaining about it?

I had a face-to-face conversation with Beetle Bailey, our Florida OFR area supervisor, when he was a field examiner and asked if he was being selected to replace the retiring area supervisor. He said that he had only seventeen years with the agency, was the junior person, and not in line for promotion. He was promoted to area supervisor a few weeks later. Whether he was uninformed or just lied to me, I don't know.

Beetle Bailey sat in my office and talked incoherently for 1 hour 50 minutes one afternoon. He did not allow the other person, a subordinate and the examiner-in-charge for that examination, to speak.

He did that with such regularity that my executive leadership team used to come into my office and say they'd just spent an hour with him and had no idea what he said. At the end of the 1 hour 50 minutes, I asked if that was the exit interview? "No," he replied. "I will drive back to Tampa and then schedule a return trip to waste more resources and your time," he said. "We are required to return later to conduct an exit interview."

"Pray tell," said I, "what will you say that you did not say in the last 1 hour 50 minutes?"

"Nothing," he said, "but it is a rule."

"May I sign something today that verifies we had the exit interview and spare all of us the repetitive actions and additional expense," I asked.

"No, we have rules," he said.

Beetle reported to his boss, Fred Flintstone, that I refused to participate in an exit interview. Coming from someone who falsely complained about their salary, and placed the blame at the feet of his boss in Tallahassee for incorrect findings that cannot be revised, it was totally in character for him to do so.

On another occasion, when informed that I had a planned vacation and would not be available, old Beetle said to me, "Don't make me come back here, or we will assess your organization double for the examination."

There is a little-known Florida Statute that allows the FLORIDA OFR to assess an additional fee for examinations under certain conditions. That has never been enforced, and more importantly, the person who issued the threat has no authority to impose it.

When I reported his conduct to Fred Flintstone, I was assured FLORIDA OFR would never impose the additional expense. My board wanted that incident to be part of our response to the examination. I was lambasted by Fred for writing our objection to his employees' unsatisfactory behavior and threat.

He said, "I told you we would never assess your credit union an additional examination fee"

I responded, "Yes, but I have heard many lies from FLORIDA OFR over the years, and our board of directors instructed me to record our objection."

To err is human, to err humble is divine. We were not even in the ball park with divine.

Fred Flintstone raised his voice to me via telephone for purportedly refusing to participate in an exit interview and for including our written objection to any additional exam expense. He attempted to recover from his misstep by telling me he was one of us because he had sat on the other side of the desk. I am not certain when that occurred, nor was his comment applicable to how he was acting.

But hey, Fred Flintstone was making a bunch of money and had virtually no one to answer to, so there were no consequences for whatever he decided to do or how he chose to act.

The take away is that leading with integrity sends a powerful message to employees. Personal accountability and clarity are essential to leadership. Leadership by example is the crux of creating an environment and culture where integrity is a shared virtue throughout any organization or government agency. Integrity matters.

But integrity wasn't part of the FLORIDA OFR culture.

# Chapter 7: Leadership Responsibility

*"Character may be manifested in the great moments, but it is made in the small ones."* --- Phillip Brooks

I n any discussion of leadership, we tend to think and see leadership primarily as a privilege attached to rank or position. Leaders are not born. Leaders are developed, often one decision at-a-time. The quality of your leadership determines your future, how high you rise in an organization, the future of your organization, and the lives of all those who follow you as well as your own life.

When it comes to federal and state regulatory agencies, with a few exceptions, quality of leadership doesn't appear to matter. In the government sector, leaders are often promoted based upon seniority or appointed as a political favor. It's not because they're outstanding leaders.

Winston Churchill said, "The key to leadership is sincerity. Before he can inspire with emotion, he must be swayed by it himself. Before he can move their tears, his own must flow. To convince them, he must himself believe."

Obviously, many of those in leadership during the 2008 Banking Collapse were not of/from Churchill's school of leadership.

The behaviors and attitudes of person's in positions of leadership are learned and cultivated by experience over time. They are the tangibles that make their success, or failure, predictable. In private industry, applicants come to the job interview with a resume and references. They are prescreened for technical skills, knowledge and applicable education in the field for which they are being recruited. Few, however, are profiled for attitudes, behaviors and values. Interestingly enough, if that person is later fired, it's usually for attitude or lack of leadership. They had the education and experience—all of which were verified. But, they didn't have the skills and attitude to lead.

In regulatory agencies, too often persons are placed into positions of influence as a result of length of service. They go from being a field examiner, for example, to being a director or bureau chief. The requirements of these positions are very different, and at the elevated levels, communication skills, collaboration with others, diplomacy and a sense of social responsibility are paramount. Leadership of these agencies has failed its employees by not providing leadership training. They have in effect set-up their employees and the institutions they lead to fail.

Even more important to note is that the leadership of the regulatory agencies has failed to learn from their mistakes. They do not recognize the symbiotic relationship between the financial institutions they regulate and their agencies.

I accept that credit unions and banks cannot and should not exist without regulatory oversight. It is reasonable to expect that examiners, if doing their jobs, will ruffle some feathers. It is not reasonable to expect that the examiners goal is to kill the bird.

When you think of leadership in regulatory agencies, envision a wind sock. As the wind blows, so goes the direction of the sock. Examiners and their leaders are the modern embodiment of Chicken Little. Every issue is elevated to a major, sky-is-falling obstacle instead of an everyday challenge. The pattern is unwaveringly pessimistic, misguided and detrimental to the regulated, all in service to the few who do the regulating.

Letters from Mr. Swann, NCUA Director in Atlanta, would direct us to talk to our problem case officer (PCO) for assistance and questions. I would call Olive Oil, the problem case officer, and she would respond by saying, "I don't know what he means." Denial was the name of their game, and their plan was to run us around in circles until they could hammer us into submission.

The economy was in a state of flux and only the strong could survive, as it should be. Consumer savings rates were 4%, spending and eating out were all down. Fewer vacations and new cars were the new normal. In a business model where 75%-85% of gross income is derived from interest on loans, the shrinking margins influenced asset/liability for years to come as credit unions and banks continued to grant 72-month auto loans at 1.65% APR.

A house is a house again, not an investment. It is where we live and raise a family. No more using our home as an automated teller machine. Homes will be smaller and functional. Big boy houses, aka "mc mansions" are out. Houses over $1.0 million are often on the market for years.

Nobody is talking about this, though. Government is broke. Taxes are like crack cocaine, and they're inflated 15%.

Recessions always end. But, they also come again. The lessons of this last recession, however, have not been collected, debated and applied. The country is on the precipice of another recession, perhaps worse that the last, and yet, we still have unresolved issues and lessons we need to learn from.

Leaders in the regulatory agencies look at financial institutions under a microscope; however, they view themselves with a telescope.

Put in other terms, consider the two-sided mirror many of you have on your bathroom counter. One side is a normal view, while the flip side is 7-10X magnification. Virtually nobody looks good when magnified 10X.

That said, that is what the leadership of any organization must have the courage to do. They must look at themselves and their actions using the 10X lens. Until a leader knows him or herself to that degree and can change themselves for the better, they cannot change their organization.

With the decline in the number of credit unions and banks, one would think there may be some consequences for the regulators. But, that isn't so. As long as examination fees are based upon the footings (assets) of the regulated organizations, rather than any metrics of success, profitability, or growth, there is no reduction in income for the regulatory agencies. They are free to hire more staff and increase salary and benefits. It sounds like a Ponzi scheme, and, in an awful way, it is.

I am reminded almost every day via news reports of the actions of those in positions of trust who have violated their pledge. There are many Bernie Madoffs surviving and thriving.

In crisis management, it is an accepted practice that the offending company go public with a sincere apology, acknowledge the mistake and explain what action(s) will be taken to correct the issue. After the Gulf Oil Spill, BP did that, and we have seen that with Tylenol and other corporate giants. They demonstrated empathy via compassionate communication, were swift to accept the blame and gave an appropriate response to what happened, why it happened and what was being done to prevent it from happening again.

Government and the financial services cabal, however, are more focused on "saving face" and continuing to make profits than on taking right actions. It's ingrained in the culture of their very beings. When saving face and greed are more important than the truth, trust is destroyed. When individuals are reluctant to say anything that is not the party line or well-inside group think parameters, trust cannot exist.

An example of saving face at all costs may be seen in the NCUA. The NCUA has a three-member Board to oversee NCUA's operations. They set policy, approve budgets and make all of the rules. In 2011, NCUA relied upon 1,187 full-time equivalent employees to oversee 7,094 federally insured credit unions, representing 91.8 million members, who represented savings balances of $827.4 billion.

An increase in staff at NCUA came at a time when the number of credit unions was dramatically shrinking. In 2006, there were 8,535 credit unions (now down by 16%). By comparison, government records show that the number of employees at the NCUA rose 28 percent.

The NCUA Office of Inspector General reported in its semiannual report as of Dec. 31, 2010, NCUA was servicing 215 fewer credit unions, roughly a 3 percent decline from a year earlier—primarily because of the mergers and liquidations we previously discussed. On average, one credit union per day disappeared through mergers, forced by NCUA. Nice gig if you can get it. The regulator that oversees is the same one that forces the number of credit unions to shrink, all the while increasing the number of employees and annual budget at the NCUA.

The level of distrust between the NCUA and the credit union movement is toxic. Yet no NCUA director has been willing to simply say, "We apologize." Saving face is paramount. Along with greed.

The NCUA has only to use "safety and soundness" in a single sentence to order a credit union to be placed under one of several administrative actions. For example, in a Report of Examination, or perhaps sooner in a Document of

Resolutions, a Special Actions Examiner can write, "the credit union is operating in an unsafe and unsound manner." Whatever follows in that report is almost certain to be lethal to the credit union involved.

While they are closing credit unions and placing others under the thumb of administrative actions, employees of the NCUA, financed by the credit unions they oversee, are travelling to Japan, Italy, Ireland, Portugal, Poland and many other foreign destinations. The list includes the Mexican resort cities of Acapulco, Cancun, San Jose Del Cabo and a German ski area called Garmisch-Partenkirchen.

Evaluating the merits of those trips is difficult without all of the details. How long the trips lasted, what hotels the employees stayed in and what kinds of charges they ran up at those hotels is information that the NCUA claims it does not have or does not need to disclose.

In response to requests under the Freedom of Information Act, the NCUA provided partial travel records to JunketSleuth. The agency denied some of the information sought, asserting that some of the records were not in the agency's possession. Really?! You oversee thousands of credit unions but are not in possession of your own organization's expense accounts?

The data that the NCUA did produce showed that travel spending more than doubled between 2003 and 2010, rising from $10 million a year to $22 million a year. A 120% increase. Between 2003 and 2010, annual travel spending went from being 6.8% of the agency's overall budget to 11 percent. Travel spending increased to about 20% from 2009 to 2010. The NCUA's travel spending last year translated to nearly $21,000 per employee, one of the highest figures that JunketSleuth has seen among the federal agencies that have provided data. (Source: JunketSleuth.com, July 17, 2011)

Even the implication that the NCUA is withholding information and refusing to acknowledge mistakes is frightening. They have no accountability process, let alone a willingness to offer an authentic apology. They are unapproachable. They're above the laws and regulations they oversee.

Great leaders are accountable for themselves, and they're accountable to others. They're trustworthy. But, trust is a fragile quality. Once it's lost, it can be difficult to regain or repair.

Creating a culture of understanding, being transparent, leading by example and creating an environment of mutual respect and honesty are vital pieces of establishing trustworthiness. The NCUA and FLORIDA OFR failed all measures of trustworthiness.

Do they loathe credit unions? I do not believe that is true. They simply have no ethical values and have no consequences for their greed-driven, deviant actions. They operate based on power, and we all know, in this day and age, we can't trust most of power-players.

I recall a comparison a trusted advisor shared regarding what level of incompetency from an employee is acceptable. His illustration was a nurse who cares for newborns. The grading system was how many babies could be dropped before it was unacceptable. 1 of 10? 2 of 10? The answer, of course, was none. It's unacceptable to drop an infant, period. Yet we allow the regulatory agencies to continually make mistakes and drop all of the babies on their watch.

They create their own truths. They act improperly and do so without consequences. All actions, however, have consequences. Perhaps not in this life. But there will be a judgment day for all of us.

One of my harshest critics, a rogue, former credit union director, once proclaimed the regulatory examination process of little value, and that is from a person who was an internal auditor, CPA and fraud examiner.

When I think of the characteristics a successful examiner/regulator needs to possess, I consider curiosity, persistence, discipline, energy and compassion. The same can be said of leaders. Cynicism and a hunger for power and greed have no place in the repertoire of leaders and examiners.

If regulatory agencies were able to provide consistent, ethical and predictable decisions, it is my humble opinion that would be agreeable to most of us who they watch over. Add immediate responses to our requests and submissions, and we would have a responsible regulatory system.

What Congress and the State never intended when NCUA and FLORIDA OFR were created was that the regulatory agencies would become oppressors. A responsible regulatory system has to provide oversight, but they should be acting in the best interests of the institutions over which they have oversight.

There is a passage in Matthew 7:5 that says, and I paraphrase, 'take the beam out of your own eye, to deal with the speck in your friend's eye.' There is little doubt as to how the regulators interpret that. They will espouse that their responsibilities and authority under unchallenged laws makes them immune to introspection. No one is charged with making sure they operate with integrity, values or the wisdom from the Bible.

The regulatory agencies in this country are not only devoid of leadership, they also don't have the knowledge to effectively discharge their duties. Because of their lack of know-how, they're responsible for the demise of many organizations, and they've hindered the healing of financial institutions from one of the longest and deepest recessions the U.S. has faced.

The credit union system is being systematically strangled by its regulatory agencies. Just as credit unions were created as a social movement over 100 hundred years ago in the U.S. in response to the needs of consumers for fair prices and ethical treatment, so will another movement arise that will take the place of credit unions.

Edmund Burke, an English Philosopher, is credited with saying, "All that is necessary for evil to triumph is for good men to do nothing." There are plenty of examples of that being true during the 2008 Banking Collapse.

Will we take action, step-up, and do something? Or will we do nothing and watch history repeat itself?

Regulators, politicians and CEOs lie because we let them do so and get away with it. They know their constituencies well. We're not going to challenge their ethically questionable behavior because we believe that nothing will change. There are no consequences and no better options.

Do we even care about any of this anymore?

In almost all dealings with state and federal examiners, leadership denies, ducks, ignores the issue or simply hides behind their offices and titles. In the regulatory agencies and the institutions they watch over, there's an authority abyss, and, unfortunately, it involves credit unions, too.

The message to the next generation of credit unions and examiners is that there exists a learning opportunity. A failure of leadership doesn't have to be fatal. The half-truths and intimidation tactics used during the Collapse and still being used are simply not sustainable.

The Credit Union National Association (CUNA, Inc.), the largest association for credit unions and one of the most influential lobbying organizations in Washington, DC, published a bill of rights for credit unions in response to the regulatory climate. CUNA also had a survey of examiner issues. I requested a copy or at least permission to read it, but, because I was no longer employed in the industry, I received no reply.

Additionally, a brave group of Michigan Credit Union CEO's enumerated a list of grievances to NCUA, signed it, and sent it to the NCUA Board (December 2010). CU Times (08/08/11) reported that in April 2010 a group of Knoxville-area credit union executives presented its own "declaration of grievances" with 91 signatures. They criticized NCUA policies and called for change by lobbying Congress for swift action to prevent "catastrophe" to the industry.

On January 24, 2011, CUNA filed serious concerns with the NCUA Board's proposal to amend Part 704 regarding corporate credit unions. Part 704 establishes special rules for all federally-insured corporate credit unions. Non federally-insured corporate credit unions must agree, by written contract, to both adhere to the requirements of this part and submit to examinations, as determined by NCUA, as a condition of receiving shares or deposits from federally-insured credit unions. On March 4, 2011, CUNA opposed most of the provisions in NCUA's proposal to Part 704.

I do not wish to cast aspersions on all examiners, CEO's or boards of directors. People who decide to make a career in credit unions often do so to satisfy their altruistic need to help others. But, they often end up being angels working among devils.

# Chapter 8: Dancing with the Bear

*"Once you start dancing with a bear, you can never stop."*
--- Yitzhak Rabin (1922-1995)

Credit unions are a small portion of the financial services industry with approximately 6% of consumer deposits in the United States.

In good economic times, the regulators are harmless, much like giving an enema to a dead person. However, they can be the bear that credit unions have to dance with, making them dangerous and unpredictable.

Act like an adult if you want to be treated and respected as one. Sounds reasonable, doesn't it? Yet if the leadership of an organization does not demand that of its employees or exhibit that behavior itself, there will be no consequences when adults act like 4-year olds.

Case in point...

Fred Flintstone, Chief, Bureau of Credit Union Regulation, said to me, "You really don't respect examiners do you?"

My reply was, "No Sir, I do not."

Want to be liked, show some like for the other person; want to be respected, show some respect.

There are a lot of distasteful things and people in the world, and two that really get under my skin are bullies and liars. In my experience, they are the same and take the form of NCUA and FLORIDA OFR examiners.

Communication is as important in business as it is in marriage. And, all you married folks will agree that often it's the non-verbal communication—posture, facial expressions, dress and appearance—that ends up being most powerful. Leaders that are poor communicators often express their personal thoughts verbally and non-verbally. But, there's no written record of the non-verbal antics. Thus, personal accountability is lost, and they can deny having said or done anything wrong.

For example, Beetle Bailey would suggest that we take some insignificant action that was intended to make his job easier, but was of no value to the credit union. And, it was the way in which he communicated his intentions that made them come across as much more than suggestions.

Too many examiners, CEO's and board members act like Beetle Bailey in ways that would sadden their Mama and St. Peter.

How did the credit union movement misplace its integrity and basic human decency? When did it become okay to tell untruths? How did it become acceptable to the rest of us? Do we place greater importance on a borrower's character for a car loan than we require from each other? And, why is that more important than eliminating the trend of banks setting themselves up too big to fail?

CUNA reported, "For better or worse, the trend toward fewer but larger CUs continues. The gradual but incessant migration toward fewer but larger credit unions continues, apparently unimpeded by economic ups and downs."

The State and NCUA regulatory bodies are unaffected by the shrinkage in the movement, as are CUNA and the State Leagues, for so long as dues income and/or exam fees are determined by assets and/or the number of members, it's in their best interests for merger mania to continues.

According to the World Council of Credit Unions, Madison, Wisconsin (WOCCU), at their peak in 1969, there were 23,900 U.S. credit unions. 'If this trend continues--and likely it will--there will be fewer than 11,000 credit unions by the year 2000.' (Source: Steven W. Rick, Credit Union National Association February 27, 1998)

By 2010, there were 7,708 credit unions in the U.S., and that's down to roughly 5,000 in March 2017. By comparison, in Canada, there were 945, in 2009. That country has been moving to fewer, larger national credit unions for some time. And, I think we are right behind them.

Mergers used to come about because a credit union CEO was retiring, not because of NCUA's zealousness and hostile takeovers. Those were not shotgun weddings, but rather, a voluntary consolidation where the merging credit union staff was treated fairly. The departing CEO may be offered a job in the surviving credit union or put to pasture with a financial settlement befitting their contributions he or she made over a long career. The next merger partner is going to want to talk to the last consummated merger CEO.

Today's mergers are likely to be initiated by NCUA and its staff. The management of the merged credit union are kicked to the curb, contracts voided, cultures destroyed and no value added as a result.

A study cited that in 80% of all mergers, no additional value was created, and in 50% of all mergers, value was actually destroyed. Mergers do little to add value for the surviving organization or its stakeholders. Yet, the trend continues.

NCUA uses mergers to bury problematic organizations—problematic because they're well-run and are making money, which makes the bigger banks make less than they potentially could. Or, problematic because on account of the housing bubble that burst they were failing miserably. They also do nothing to address the root causes of the institutions who are operating at a loss-which are the expensive, burdensome, strangling regulations that are so risk adverse that progress and recovery isn't allowed.

Mergers as a part of a growth strategy are appropriate. The plans, however, have to at least address the Board's position on mergers. Since a majority of credit unions are not growing members organically, a merger that strengthens your field of membership, and is a good fit culturally, should be on the table.

Determining that the cultures of the proposed merger participants are compatible is overlooked, unverified, and in most cases, not even a consideration. Some mergers come about because the two CEO's played golf and decided that their respective organizations were alike and the cultures were a match. Giving your golf buddy two strokes a side does not constitute a culture match. For example, I was wined and dined several times, including a golf trip at the TPC Sawgrass course by our first suitor.

Regulators at the state level have never seen a merger application they did not like, providing the surviving organization remains a state-chartered credit union and the state's exam fees are not decreased as a result.

That was true of our initial merger partner. Alas, that CEO and Board revealed their true character and intent in time for my board chair to cancel. The pressures were mounting on me, however, to select a merger candidate. But, most of my choices in Florida were also experiencing heavy loan losses and were thus ineligible.

That compounded the challenges and forced me to invite an unknown CEO, who had about eight months on the job, to negotiate. I took the bait, completely. He prayed before meals, told me he had followed my career for years, and we shared common acquaintances. I recall him telling me I should talk to folks in the state where he had been before coming to Florida to verify his character. That is someone trying to say, "I ain't lying".

After the merger, as my job searches evolved, I was in his previous state and did ask a few what they thought of him. The information was too late. Those that knew him said his management style was 'my way or the highway'. I was told that he considered a run for the state house of representatives, but could not secure the backing and endorsement of that state's credit union league. At a time when the tensions between the banking lobbies and credit union lobbies were at a pitched fanaticism, most state leagues (the associations of all credit unions in a state formed for lobbying and governmental affairs) would have welcomed just about any warm body without a felony arrest, especially if they were opposing a banker running for elected office.

Credit unions involved in mergers used to simply blend the balance sheets and the chips would fall where they may. Today, credit unions with over $10 million in assets are required to follow GAAP (Generally Accepted Accounting Principles) which required specialized accounting for quite a while in banking, but changed a few years ago for mutual organizations, including credit unions. Before the codification, the rule was called SFAS 141R, but now it's called ASC 820.

So, the surviving credit union will invest tens of thousands of dollars to establish the amount of "goodwill" it will book, and annually have to verify, but it will not invest a dime to validate that the cultures of the two organizations are compatible and the merger will add value?

I was a credit union executive for 29 years, the last 25 as a CEO, and I have participated in five mergers. None of them ever tried to measure that the cultures were a match. It was all about GAAP.

What does an ethical merger look like?

The CEO's of two credit unions agree, with the approval of both Boards, to conduct due diligence and develop a plan for success and present it in 90-days.

In reality, though, here's what most look like, including mine...

The surviving CEO and Chairman of the Board promises on multiple occasions to the merging Board that two (2) directors will be seated on the Board of the surviving organization to provide local representation in as much as they're located about 100 miles away. That promise is rescinded with no explanation. That becomes a deal breaker because of the suspicion of trust going forward.

A possible solution would be for the surviving CEO to bow out and agree to both Boards sitting down and discussing the issue. In principle, having the CEO's as the point for negotiations makes sense, however, it is the Board who has the fiduciary responsibility. It's often a slippery slope when a CEO announces that they speak for their Board, as many I have negotiated with have done. Arrogance and ego clouds judgment.

The organization we ended up being forced to merge with was unfamiliar with the challenges they would encounter with a large merger. They had completed several mergers in which the merged organization was less than $10 million in assets. We were about $245 million.

Hubris clouded reason and e-mails with inaccurate information created an environment of doubt that the surviving CEO had the competency to manage this merger. The potential surviving CEO never did call me, the merging

CEO, to try to work through the issues; nor did the surviving CEO realize that simply combining the balance sheets was no longer permissible.

So here we were…two CEO's, instructed by their respective Boards to negotiate in good faith and come back with a plan for approval. Regrettably, there wasn't much good faith. Egos got in the way of good dialogue. Morality is needed to manage ego and to let in a little humility.

An attorney, who had never negotiated a credit union merger, wrote unenforceable and dubious language in a severance and consultancy agreement. He had no prior relationship with the surviving CEO, who himself had never negotiated a merger and his CFO had no credit union experience,

On a conference call, during which my attorney was present, I said I did not have a draft of the agreement to which they referred. Both yelled…and I mean yelled…that it had been emailed to my attorney and me. Neither of us had received it. When we finally did, questionable language said:

1) personal dishonesty resulting in gain to or personal enrichment of Executive at XXX's expense;
2) incompetence, insubordination, misconduct or conduct unbecoming of a senior credit union officer which negatively reflects upon XXX;
3) breach of fiduciary duty;
4) failure to perform the duties stated in this Agreement;
5) violation of any law, rule, or regulation (other than minor traffic violations or similar offenses);
6) violation of a final cease-and-desist order; and/or
7) personal default on indebtedness, which is not corrected within 30 days from the date of default.

When asked about this, the surviving CEO replied, "We will never enforce that language so why don't you just sign it?" He and his lawyer in Tallahassee slipped the clauses into the proposed consultancy agreement. They're not legally enforceable, and, frankly, were an insult.

Attorneys agree that your employer cannot legally fire you because you are 30 days in arrears or have filed for bankruptcy. The personal dishonesty, incompetence, etc., were and are personally offensive and disregarded my entire career and life. I did not agree and refused to sign the agreement.

There are so many things wrong with the language proposed I scarcely know where to start, e.g.; if it isn't legally enforceable, and if you will never enforce it, why is it in the agreement? And this was supposed to be a friendly merger. After all, the surviving credit union was invited to the table to begin with.

When negotiating for continued group major medical insurance, the answer was, "We don't provide coverage for retirees. Why don't you go to the Veteran's Administration like my father?"

*Note: Under the Consolidated Omnibus Budget Reconciliation Act of 1985, commonly referred to as COBRA, you and your family have the right to retain access to your employer-provided group health insurance for up to 18 months after you leave the job. That means you will get the same coverage and the same doctors you have now. You will have to pay for 100% of the coverage, rather than sharing the cost with your employer, but it's still usually cheaper than buying an equivalent policy on your own.*

I asked him why he did not return my calls. Why he was upset and being difficult. He replied that his unmarried, adult daughter was pregnant, and he placed all blame upon her boyfriend, whom he disliked. I said I was sorry to hear that, but it was not my problem, nor relevant to the merger.

The surviving CEO made the statement to my executive leadership team that he was new in his position, had no allegiance to his staff as he did not hire them, and, going forward, it was his intent to form the best team, and so, everyone would be considered. That statement was also made in the presence of the merger leader on his team.

Ego both fosters and destroys. Ego wants you to believe that you are your job, your title, your material possessions, and that you are smarter, better looking, and above all else, that you are right about everything.

Credit Unions have a lot of latitude in merger negotiations, so they need to be done in good faith, or not at all. That said, they can be smooth and effective transitions, if done right.

In the case examples I just gave you, the Boards of Directors were not involved. All the rules of negotiations were ignored and emotions consumed all common sense.

At the time, we had already identified other merger candidates and our attorney said to me, "Let me carry your briefcase (and attend the meeting) when you go see the next Credit Union CEO".

And I'm glad he did...

The powers at the Bureau of Credit Union Regulation made it a stipulation of the merger that all details of my severance agreement must be published in the newspaper, approved by them, and sent to all 26,000 members via U.S. mail. The terms of said severance had been approved by two independent boards of directors, both CEOs, and both attorneys for the parties.

Legal counsel advised the Chief of the Bureau of Credit Union Regulation that the local newspaper was certain to publish the terms, and, of course, they did because the employees of that paper were members of the credit union. It was 15 minutes of embarrassment and had no effect on the voting by the membership on the merger.

According to the credit union's legal counsel, there is no requirement to publish the details of what had been approved by the boards of directors. The letter detailed all the financial arrangements of my salary, retirement, etc. It was retaliation for my past grievances with the Chief of the Bureau of Credit Union Regulation.

Jimmy Mack was a full-time financial contractor in Jacksonville for the Florida Division of Financial Services and a law student earning $45.00 per hour. I never met or spoke to him. He was ordered to sign the letter and was used as a pawn. Fred Flintstone, Chief, Bureau of Credit Union Regulation, was the person with the authority calling the shots, and he was a chicken shit who delegated the job so that the stink didn't get on him.

Here is the information that neither the FLORIDA OFR nor the surviving organization disclosed to our membership that had to approve or disapprove this merger:

We, like hundreds of banks and other credit unions, were not profitable at the time of the merger due to extraordinary loan losses. The surviving organization was allowed to book $20 million in goodwill and use any amount needed from that sum to pay for severance packages, and other merger costs, so none of those expenses ran through their P&L.

In addition, they acquired $10.0 million in reserves and after loan losses in the acquired loan portfolio, we (the merged credit union), showed net profits of over $1.0 million in the 4th quarter of 2009.

None of that information was disclosed to the stakeholders of the organization. The newspaper did not have that information. No mention was made or disclosed that the surviving organization assumed insurance policies on me with a cash value of $3.9 million, paying 5% per year, which offset my severance package nearly five times. I was vilified by many for receiving my supplemental retirement, in which I was vested and had legally binding agreements to receive.

I was portrayed as a greedy bastard who had run the organization into the ground and was walking away with a big severance package. Not only is that not true, the narrow requirement of the FLORIDA OFR with the complicity of the surviving organization to disclose my severance amount without any frame of reference does not pass the smell test. This was business as usual, not just my case.

The board of directors of both organizations had a legal obligation that compelled them to honor my 20 years of service and retirement benefits, some of which was money I'd fully vested.

What I was forced to do is reveal in the newspaper, and in a letter to all stakeholders, including all my employees, the sum total of my personal retirement benefits. When grossed-up to pay the payroll taxes on the lump sum, you bet your sweet ass it was a significant amount.

The eventual outcome may have been the same and the vote unchanged; however, there would have been context to the legal obligations of my board of directors honoring an employment agreement and a 457 Plan guaranteed by a Rabbi Trust. (In the United States, a Rabbi Trust is a type of trust used by businesses or other entities to defer the taxability to the person or entity receiving (the payee) such payments as employee compensation or purchase payments in the acquisition of another business.)

Neither the FLORIDA OFR, NCUA nor the surviving organization sought to clarify that the merger was voluntary. That it was an economic crisis, not a management event. Or, to apologize to me and my family for dragging us through the mud in a very public fashion. The implication was that I had failed, when, in point of fact, we had in writing the problem case officer's comments that this was an economic crisis, NOT a management event. I was not allowed to include her comments in the published letter or to my beloved staff.

The surviving organization made the decision to pay my retirement in a lump sum, rather than deposit an amount annually or monthly on my behalf, which I would have preferred. They requested that I consult my insurance, accounting and legal advisers and submit an amount—to include all applicable taxes that would be due—to them, and from the $20 million in goodwill that they booked; I would be paid so they could be done with me.

The surviving CEO has no idea how close he came to failing to close the deal. The only reason we did not terminate the letter of intent and negotiate with another was that we had done so with the first potential partner and the time and expense to begin anew was too great. In the end, we settled for an undesirable partner, a confirmed liar, and with no common culture or shared values.

Cultures need to be authentic across all delivery channels. If the CEO, board of directors, or examiners and their leaders, cannot be truthful, genuine and model the behaviors that send positive messages throughout their respective organizations, whose responsibility is it? The surviving CEO? Or the one who agreed to make him/her the only survivor? I've pondered this question many times over the years.

An alternative would be to retain a third-party mediator so the process may be managed in a collaborative manner. Both organizations could use the same attorney and CPA, with appropriate industry experience and references. That would reduce the duplication of expenses, remove the egos of competing professionals and provide both boards of directors a single source of information and counsel.

The surviving organization retained one executive from our organization, and she left at the end of one year. During the months following the merger, no senior executive of the surviving organization visited the merged organization, and they required all meetings to be attended 45 miles away. The merged stakeholders lost the personal touch and sense of family. The surviving organization continues to refer to the merged organization as "the south division." That designation will not create a unified sense of family and ownership.

Even though it's subtle, the staff and members of the merged organization feel and see it and it does zilch to build trust and collaboration. Even member surveys were coded "south" in the upper left corner of the return envelope. The promise was to create one organization, not a territory or a sphere of activity that is controlled by a particular person or group.

New fees were slipped in at the time of merger. The lines of members closing their memberships were literally out the door at the merged credit union's locations. Value was not created, it was destroyed.

The $20 million goodwill value of the merged institution was determined, in part, by its brand, reputation and culture. To destroy the brand, change the name and not retain the very people that created the value seems shortsighted. Most successful airline and other industry mergers retain the brand of the merged organization as part of a new company identity. Many credit unions have done so by leaving the name and brand intact, and adding a line that says "a subsidiary of XXX FCU."

So much for accountability and clarity. I was deprived of either as was my organization.

# Chapter 9: Situational Ethics

*"Life is mostly froth and bubble; Two things stand like stone: Kindness in another's trouble, Courage in our own."*
--- Adam Lindsay (Lionel Gordon) Gordon

It has been suggested in the writings of Stanley Hauerwas that any truth that requires force to maintain is not a truth. He said that all ethics come from a meticulous story about life, and that all ethics come from a specific narrative about life, and the term ethics requires a modifier...whose ethics are we discussing?

If Hauerwas was right, there is no universal right or wrong. Instead, there's a tribal right or wrong. In other words, our understanding of right or wrong is culturally conditioned by the storyline from which we operate. That may be why we find the people who live in our story endlessly making efforts to modify the narrative. The turf struggles and power games we witness can leave anyone baffled about what is right and wrong.

We share a common language. But, we use different dictionaries. Fearing you may think that only state and federal credit union regulators and their appointed leaders are capable of inventing their own truth, let's dispel that. I have never known anyone, including myself, who hasn't manipulated another to achieve their own goals. And most of us wish we could have a do-over on some decisions we've made and actions we've taken.

In order for leaders to become aware of what is going on in their organizations, which allows them to provide values and harmony, they must be asking the correct questions of the right people. And using the same dictionaries. That's seldom done. Most executives listen only to their staff and that causes a head-in-the-sand effect.

Being a leader is not a part-time job. You have to be on all the time. With responsibility comes power and obligations. Leaders have to be engaged and listen to sources other than their staff. Great leaders are truly authentic people who listen more than they speak. A leader is not a title or a role you play just sometimes. A leader is who you are and how you live every day.

Ron Stebelton blogged, "If the Horse You Are Riding Dies…Get Off! If it isn't working…STOP!" That's not the same as quitting. It's an acknowledgement that you need to stop doing the same things when they are not working. In other words, get another horse and keep riding.

I include the elected volunteer directors in the definition of leaders for this discussion. They are considered officers by the regulatory agencies and have fiduciary responsibilities under state and federal regulations. In banks, directors are usually paid to attend meetings of the board and committees, thus there are a lot more meetings. Directors may be sued, and for that reason, all financial institutions provide directors & officer's liability insurance coverage.

Being a volunteer director in a credit union is sometimes a lifetime post. It is not unheard of for directors to serve for 30, 40, or 50 years on a credit union board of directors. It is wonderful to find persons with the altruistic spirit to serve without pay for the purpose of helping their fellow members.

Don't be totally naïve, though. It's not the dinner each month, but the annual trips to Las Vegas, Hawaii, London and other fantastic locations that keeps them coming back every three years. Board meeting dinners and planning session's aside, taking your spouse to the Big Island on an all-expense paid trip is tall cotton.

Directors can tell pretty lies, too. It may be situational ethics, or inadvertent, but the reason doesn't matter when you're on the receiving end. Those lies find their way into the culture of the organization and its boardroom.

Cases in point...

A selection committee comprised of members of the board interviews candidates for the position of CEO of their organization. They tell those candidates that "We will make a decision in two weeks and notify you." Three months pass without notification, and you read the position was filled. Do you want to work for a board that has this much difficulty staying true to their word?

Another example is that of the CEO of a large credit union that said to me after an interview for a C-level position, "We don't want to jerk you around, so call us back in 30-days." I did, only to be told that there was no decision, and to call back in 30-days and speak to someone else. I did, and the VP-Human Resources didn't know that the CEO had decided not to do the search in-house and had hired a consultant. I was told I would have to start fresh with the consultant. Do you want to work for a CEO that has this much difficulty staying true to their word?

# Chapter 10: Are You a Victim?

*"A good head and a good heart are always a formidable combination"* --- Nelson Mandela

You may be thinking that I need some cheese and crackers with my whine. Let me be very clear...I am NOT a victim. This is not an exercise in blaming others, nor a long-winded narrative to conceal my own shortcomings. My primary responsibility as CEO was to be a steward for the needs of the members and to deliver to the next generation an ongoing organization. In that I failed and will be haunted to my death. I believe I did my best for 29 years and in the end, it was in God's hands.

It is my position that NCUA and FLORIDA OFR believe themselves to be the victims. They feel they are innocent in every situation. They cannot or will not hold themselves accountable. Everyone else is at fault. These folks get stuck in the injured party mode, e.g.: "my pay is too low; you don't respect us; there's nothing I can do about that; or, all I can do is wait and see what Atlanta or Tallahassee says." They live in a world of denial. Their credibility is gone, and they pretend not to know there's a problem or that they are the problem.

Research indicates that about 60-70% of persons asked do not know their company's vision, let alone how their actions or work affects that vision. Regrettably, state and federal regulatory and many human services agencies make little effort to align their plans, resources, and staff through a vision statement.

FLORIDA OFR and NCUA are, in many ways, like the Department of Families and Children (DFCS). The news is usually bad, there is unqualified leadership, the employees are unhappy, too many mistakes are made and they are managed by a revolving door of political appointees lacking the skills and knowledge or the attitudes and behavior required to be successful. Long-tenured staff makes a mess of the daily processes, but like cockroaches, they survive for eons.

Regulators, DFCS, and the Justice Department all share a culture that says you are presumed to be guilty, unless proven innocent. Their cultures have been influenced by a focus on current events instead of long-term planning and logic and a group mentality. Group mentality or 'group-think' has led to events such as the Challenger disaster (when a group refused to accept that at low temperature O-rings may fail and nobody had the guts to speak up in a group), and it's also led to events such as the 2008 Banking Collapse.

Humans and lemmings are disposed to follow the crowd. CEOs follow other CEOs; examiners follow other examiners; credit unions follow other credit unions, etc.

In a sense, we're all victims, meaning, we're also the only ones who can refuse to be victims.

# Chapter 11: Treating the Symptoms

*"Service to a just cause rewards the worker with more real happiness and satisfaction than any other venture in life."* -
-- Carrie Chapman Catt

C redit unions and banks have evolved much faster than the regulatory agencies. The financial services industry has changed with the times, adapted to regulatory demands, technology and grown.

Federal and state regulatory agencies have sweeping authority; however, it's not absolute.

For example, NCUA's negligence charges against WesCorp's 11 directors were dismissed by a federal judge. WesCorp failed in 2009 because of actions by NCUA. NCUA is suing the Royal Bank of Canada US (RBC) over its participation in the purchase of mortgage-backed securities (MBS) that WesCorp purchased in conformity with NCUA's rules. (Credit Union Journal Daily Briefing, Monday, August 1, 2011)

RBC's U.S. operation has $27.6 billion in deposits and 5,000 employees; while RBC Canada (NYSE, TSX: RX) has 79,000 employees, generated a net profit in 2010 of C$5.2 billion and is the fifth largest bank in North America. In a global economy, NCUA is to RBC as is a gnat on an elephant's ass. I'd bet RBC has a large legal department, audit and securities review specialists that will tie up NCUA a long time.

The 3-person board of directors of NCUA must have trouble keeping their pants from falling down, judging by the number of times they've have had their butts handed to them. Their conduct, along with that of FLORIDA OFR, raises questions. But most of those questions have gone unanswered and unchallenged.

NCUA asked credit unions to contribute $3.0 billion to make up a cash shortfall as a result of their own actions to conserve the corporate credit unions. They created the cash shortfall and claimed that any payment to be made was voluntary. They also claimed that failure to make these "bail-out" payments by any credit union would in no way alter examination ratings.

Given their lack of transparency and refusals to provide data that may support the request and their past actions, how can anyone believe them? I certainly did not and neither did almost any of my fellow credit union CEOs.

On August 2, 2011, NCUA announced the cancellation of the voluntary prepaid assessment funding for the temporary corporate credit union stabilization fund after only 11%, or about 800 out of 7,300 credit unions, indicated that they would support it. Again, tenured staff at NCUA had embarrassed the board of NCUA by providing advice that led the board to an ill-advised decision.

If insanity is doing the same thing over and over expecting a different result, can we get a diagnosis and treatment plan for these folks?

On September 1, 2011, Chip Filson, President, Callahan & Associates, wrote an article describing in detail NCUA's demands that credit unions bail out the Agency's $2 billion cash management shortfall of corporate assets. In a turn of events, the Agency admits that failure to make timely payment of principal and interest under NCUA's guarantee could result in "possible erosion in public confidence in the full faith and credit backing of the U.S. Government." Chip went on to say that NCUA has not been transparent and no current financial information has been provided.

What is clear is that NCUA has proven that it does not have the character or the capacity to manage its responsibilities and has taken on more than it can handle. Their flawed conclusion that credit unions should bail them out of their incompetence came at a time when credit unions were struggling and the assessment was the biggest one time hit, ever. Their employees believe themselves to be the victim, as seen by their complaints of salary, travel and lack of control of the examination process. They attempted to deflect responsibility by lodging lawsuits and issuing threats.

NCUA became so perplexed that immediate past chair Debbie Matz finally owned up that NCUA staff was spending the vast majority of their time in credit unions that hold just 10% of the total assets. That took resources from the ones who needed it in a misguided attempt to mitigate losses in the credit unions deemed "too large to fail".

Past actions are a predictor of future behavior. Credit unions, and their trade associations, have not shown a willingness to oppose coercion by NCUA and FLORIDA OFR's. To be fair, it's hard to do. But, that doesn't mean it can't be done. And until it is, our trust in them will remain shattered.

# Chapter 12: Wrapping Up

*"Those who don't know the true value of loyalty can never appreciate the cost of betrayal"* --- Unknown

I have learned that devastating actions can be both motivational and overcome. With the loss of anything, or anyone you love, time takes away the sting and permits us to process the event and take solace and inspiration from it. God will heal the hole in your heart, if you allow it to be healed.

I was naïve, duped by persons in positions of authority, and mistakenly gave too much trust to a few. Believing in others, wanting to be helpful to others and seeking to do the right thing are not values shared by all. Despite the fact that there are 2.5 billion Christians in the world and the Doxology is sung more often than Happy Birthday, some people do lie, cheat, steal, and tolerate others that do. Saying grace before a meal does not assure that a person has a non-negotiable set of beliefs and values. Nor does saying that you will never lie to someone if you, at the same time, disregard the lies told to you by others.

I intend to remain a trusting person and look for the good in people. The redhead says I'm too trusting. I believe that most persons are honest and do not try to take advantage. Most of us had honor and integrity and positive influences instilled in our formidable years. Being an adult and going out into the world to learn a skill and then earn a living should not require abandoning those values. No matter how high you climb the ladder of success, the situation, or circumstances, honesty and integrity have to be an integral part of your values and guide your conduct.

During the time that I worked on this book, I grew as a person, a Christian and a citizen. I admit that I am guilty of preconceived notions and a lack of sensitivity lens through which I view examiners. That is healing to me, and I hope a powerful example for you.

With this book, I want to start a conversation. I hope you will take my story to your next staff meeting as a place to begin to make the changes that need to be made.

On October 22, 1925, Mahatma Gandhi wrote that a fair friend wanted readers of Young India to know the seven social sins:

1. Politics without principles
2. Wealth without work
3. Pleasure without conscience
4. Knowledge without character
5. Commerce without morality
6. Science without humanity
7. Worship without sacrifice

Gandhi wrote, "Naturally, the friend does not want the readers to know these things merely through the intellect but to know them through the heart so as to avoid them."

Ours may be the only civilization since the Roman Empire that teaches 'pleasure without conscience' and to excuse 'knowledge without character.'

We collectively ignore violations of the honor code, and we don't teach our children that it is NOT okay to bully or disrespect others, lie, cheat, steal, or tolerate those who do. We have become numb to bad news and lack of civility, honor and integrity. Politician's model unsatisfactory behaviors almost daily. Leaders lie with impunity. We watch and tolerate it.

We tolerate it from the examiners, and we tolerate it from each other.

Leadership, truth, civility, honor and integrity are values upon which our nation was founded. I have no expectation that we will rediscover those values, however, I reject any notion that these values are inappropriate in business, the regulatory systems or any enterprise or institution.

I am worried about my country, my former industry and your children and grandchildren. There needs to be a sense of urgency and a civil discussion taking place. I don't see any organization with the cojones to step up and start it.

How about you and your organization?

Got values?

Got an honor code?

And are you willing to enforce them?

# PART II: LEADERSHIP LESSONS: A STUDY GUIDE

**Discussion starters for you and your organization**

1. Are you forcing it?

(Instincts come naturally. If you have to ponder for days whether something is really the right move, maybe you're forcing something that's not in your best interest.)

2. What is really important to you today?

3. What are you willing to change to achieve it?

4. What are you willing to give up in order to achieve it?

5. It is not a sign of weakness to admit wrongdoing and to apologize. In fact, it enhances your reputation and authority.

6. Is the adage "if you are not part of the solution, you are part of the problem" applicable?

7. When the facts do not support the request, what should you do?

8. What can NCUA and FLORIDA OFR do to regain their professional status and trust?

9. How do we assess NCUA's and FLORIDA OFR's erratic behavior and shady ethics?

10. If boards and management made their concerns known to the regulators in significant numbers, would it matter?

11. Do you seek to understand and listen or do you just like to hear yourself talk?

12. As a leader, are you engaged? How so?

13. What effect does your ego have on leadership and truth?

14. What would be the effect if you sought advice from parties other than your staff?

15. When leaders fail is that an indicator of role confusion or dissatisfaction?

16. Would you accept a behavior in question from your children or subordinates?

17. Why is that behavior acceptable coming from regulators and other credit unions?

18. How does 'it's my way or the highway' leadership styles shape staff confidence?

19. Is that style of manager even relevant today?

20. Peter Drucker said, "Leadership is all about results." What is the risk if results are gained at any cost? Or, if inappropriate results are the outcome?

21. When leadership fails to set the tone and demands honesty, who is to blame?

22. Is leadership a verb or a noun to you?

23. What is the difference between being right and being effective?

24. Is self-esteem battered so that we are not motivated to develop?

25. Has our country, and your organization, reached the point that we have learned not to trust?

26. Was it the stress of the recession and economic conditions that contributed to incivility?

27. Would your behavior and decisions be different if you applied the Four-Way Test?

28. If an organization lacks faith, vision and values, how does it influence behaviors and attitudes?

29. Does your organization have clearly defined values?

30. Which are negotiable to justify your objectives? Why?

31. If an organization has no core values, what are the possible outcomes? Does it matter what those core values are, or that its leadership has not defined any?

32. Did we relinquish honesty and accountability in the name of a bad economy? Is it really that cheap?

33. How can you have faith in a regulatory system that lacks competency in an industry they are charged with overseeing?

34. The honor code at most universities and military academies is, "I will not lie, cheat or steal, or tolerate those who do." What is your honor code?

35. If regulators cannot manage their own budget and are oblivious to the economic realities in the country, what confidence can we have in them?

36. What kind of organization would you expect if everyone in it thought and behaved the same way?

# Appendix A

*Credit Union Committee On*
*Declaration of Grievances*

March 4, 2011

Senate Banking Committee
House Financial Services Committee
2129 Rayburn House Office Building
Washington, DC 20515

RE: Declaration of Grievances – Regulatory Treatment of
Credit Unions

Dear,

The undersigned credit union CEO's and senior managers
representing many of the nation's credit unions would like
to address several critical issues affecting the 7,400 credit
unions and the 91 million American citizens and taxpayers
they serve.

We have enclosed our Declaration of Grievances along with
supporting information as representative of our complaints
that are suppressing the financial condition of our taxpaying
members and undermining the financial system that exist to
serve them. Many of these grievances are in regards to the
sufficiency of the National Credit Union Administration's
actions in regulating the industry and the many federal
agencies that are undermining our member citizens. It is our
desire and hope that you will affect the needed changes in

the many areas we have addressed for the sake of millions of Americans that are feeling the results of recent actions by these agencies.

The attached list of credit union CEO's and senior managers have signed in agreement with this
Declaration of Grievances and respectfully request attention to be given to each of these items.

Page 1

We the undersigned committee are in support of this Credit Union Declaration of Grievances:

•Rick Mikels, CEO, ETMA Federal Credit Union, rmikels@etmafcu.net
•Rhonda Sanders, CEO, LMPCOCU, lmpcocu@aeneas.net
•David Proffitt, CEO Alcoa Tenn Federal Credit Union, dproffitt@atfcu.com
•Dan Mitchell, SVP Alcoa Tenn Federal Credit Union, dmitchell@atfcu.com
•Ben Mauldin, VP Alcoa Tenn Federal Credit Union, bmauldin@atfcu.com
•Lois Profili, CEO First Eagle FCU, lprofili@firsteaglefcu.org
•Dan Sheetinger, CEO NeVista Federal Credit Union, dsheetinger@nuvista.org
•Max Griggs, CEO, Dixie Line Credit Union traindixie@aol.com
•Sandra Griffis, CEO, Illinois Central Employees Credit Union, sandragriffis@bellsouth.net
•Carter Ridgway, CEO Kemba Delta FCU, cridgway@kembadelta.org

- Gerd Henjes, CEO Countryside FCU, ghenjes@countryside.org
- Denise Cooper, CEO Upper Cumberland FCU, dcooper@ucfcu.org
- Brian Dever, CEO, PIAS Credit Union, bdever@piascu.org
- Pam Tenpenny, CEO Life Credit Union, pam@lifecu.org
- Cindy Beck, CEO KNSECU, cindy.knsecu@comcast.net
- Fara Hall, CEO Patriot Equity Credit Union, fhall@pecujax.org
- Jean Eason, Manager Parkridge Credit Union, prcu@bellsouth.net
- Mark Creech, CEO, Lowland Credit Union, bmontgomery@chcu.com
- Amy Webb, CEO, Sears Federal Credit Union, awebb@searsfcu.org
- Sherri Brooks, CEO Tennessee Employees Credit Union, sbrooks@tnecu.org
- Douglas Wilkerson, President RTP Federal Credit Union, Wilkerson@rtpfcu.org
- Lin Winkler, Shelby County Credit Union, lkwinkler@shelbycountycu.com
- Becca Montgomery, CEO Covenant Health Credit Union, bmontgomery@chcu.com
- Cynthia Appling, CEO, DuPont Memphis Plan Employees Credit Union, cappling@dmpecu.com
- Linda Morris, CEO, Bulab Employees Federal Credit Union, lhmorris@buckman.com
- Janet Tidwell, CEO Holston Methodist Federal Credit Union, jtidwell@hmfcu.org
- Lisa Hooper, CEO, McKee Credit Union, lisamckeecu@cunturytel.net
- Sam Early, Oak Ridge Schools Federal Credit Union sdearly@bellsouth.net

•Judy Mills, CEO Foothills Federal Credit Union, jmills@foothillsfcu.org
•Lynne M. Boucher, CEO Community Focus FCU, LBoucher@communityfocusfcu.org
•Henry T. Flint, Board Chair, Columbus Metro FCU, trichey@columbusmetro.org
•Tim Richey, President, Columbus Metro FCU, trichey@columbusmetro.org

Page 2

Declaration of Grievances

1. The members of federally-insured credit unions, 91 million taxpayers who are your constituents, are being drained by the recent actions of the National Credit Union Administration (NCUA) and the plethora of regulations passed by federal agencies with the delegated authority Congress has given to them (unregulated regulators). Recent actions of NCUA imposed on credit unions along with other unregulated regulators are harming each of the credit union depositors and borrowers in this country.

2. NCUA's clear failure to provide adequate supervision of the "wholesale" corporate credit unions has placed a considerable and long-term financial burden on the nation's 7,400 credit unions, which hold $748 billion in deposits of 91 million member/taxpayers. In 2010, NCUA began charging credit unions for these losses with assessments equaling approximately 27 percent of the credit unions' net income. NCUA has told the credit unions it insures to expect the aggregate assessments in 2011 to range from $1.5 to $1.9 billion. NCUA expects similar charges to the nation's credit unions and their member/taxpayers to continue through

2021–another ten years. Though these charges are applied directly to credit unions and not the American taxpayers as a whole, credit unions are cooperatives owned by our members and these charges will be borne by our member/taxpayers through reduced ownership capital, reduced savings rates, increased loan rates, increased fees, and decreased service quality.

3. While charging the nation's credit unions and their 91 million members as much as $1.9 billion in 2011, NCUA has increased its own 2011 budget by more than $24 million, passing on the expenses to each credit union during a time of recession and sacrifice for all Americans. In reality it is not the credit unions funding this 12 percent budget increase, it is the individual member/taxpayers who use credit unions to finance their daily lives. This budgetary increase by NCUA follows a similar 13 percent, $23 million budget increase in 2010.

4. The NCUA has budgeted for 78 new staff in 2011 while federally insured credit unions are downsizing and reducing expenses. This equates to a seven percent staffing increase. In addition, the NCUA Board has approved pay increases of up to eight percent for 2011 when the credit unions' member/taxpayers are experiencing little or no raises and true unemployment remains near 10 percent. Congress should require NCUA to revise its 2011 budget to 2008 levels.

5. There appears to be little or no oversight of the NCUA or any separation of powers to give balance to their actions. NCUA has closed door meetings on many occasions that are not open to the public or the scrutiny of the press. This lack of oversight has permitted NCUA to repeat past mistakes at the expense of the credit unions it regulates.

6. The Durbin Interchange Amendment as implemented by the agency will further drain the monies of credit union

member/taxpayers in the name of consumer protection. Implementation may be as soon as July 2011. The United States has the best financial payment system in the world that is being undermined by this new law. The financial services industry will lose an estimated $3.6 to $9.2 billion per year. To continue to provide efficient electronic debit and credit cards these costs will be passed on the member/taxpayer through increased cost of services. The Durbin amendment should be repealed.

7. Excessive regulations that have unintended consequences are smothering member/taxpayers with redundant notices on privacy, consumer rights notices and loan notice compliance. The current stable of Federal regulations such as the FACT Act, the SAFE Act, BSA, OFAC (to name just a few) is an incubator for costly, redundant, and often questionable notification and reporting requirements. The costs of complying with the myriad federal, state and local laws, rules and regulations are passed on to the consumer by financial institutions through increased fees, reduced interest, and increased borrowing rates. Congress and the various regulatory agencies should perform a full review of all current laws and regulations with the intent of amending or repealing those that are barriers to the free enterprise system on which this country was established and prospered. It is incumbent upon governments comprised of the people to make certain that the laws and regulations enacted and enforced upon the public are absolutely necessary and do not result in unintended harm in excess of intended good.

**NCUA's Failure to Adequately Supervise the Corporate Credit Union System**

*The Cost*

The ongoing economic turmoil has had a significant impact on the financial services industry. At first, credit unions were largely immune to the more serious ramifications being felt by many of the nation's banks. Unfortunately and as a consequence of apparent mismanagement within the four largest corporate credit unions coupled with negligence on the part of the National Credit Union Administration (NCUA), this drastically changed in 2009. Due to significant loss projections within the investment portfolios of US Central Corporate and Western Corporate credit unions (both federally-chartered corporate credit unions), NCUA moved to conserve these institutions. In addition, projected losses in the investment portfolios at Southwest Corporate and Members United Corporate (also federally chartered credit unions) resulted in their conservatorship by NCUA in 2010.

Following these conservatorships, there was an immediate cascading of losses through the corporate network and, eventually, to most of the nation's 7,400 federally-insured credit unions who, under NCUA's rules and regulations, provided the majority of the corporates' capital through uninsured capital deposits. Ultimately, the majority of the corporate credit unions became insolvent and charges of more than $2.5 billion were absorbed by their member credit unions' uninsured capital deposits. Added to these direct and immediate charges to the nation's credit unions, NCUA's loss projections will place an additional $8.3 to $10.5 billion in charges on the nation's credit unions. Credit unions have already absorbed $1.3 billion of these charges through assessments from the National Credit Union Share Insurance Fund (NCUSIF) and the remaining $7.0 to $9.2 billion will be absorbed by credit unions through 2021.

## Missed Opportunities

NCUA was clearly aware of the investment activities at these corporate credit unions for a considerable period of time. In fact, NCUA had "resident examiners" assigned to these corporates with offices on-site. These examiners were charged with monitoring all activities at the respective corporates and had full, complete and uninterrupted access to all actions, documents, records, analyses, and reports governing their investment portfolios and transactions. Even so, NCUA allowed these corporates to fail which placed a significant and long-term burden on the nation's 7,400 federally-insured credit unions and the 91 million American citizens and

taxpayers who comprise their membership.

## Déjà vu

This situation is not new to NCUA. In 1994, Capital Corporate (also a federally-chartered credit union) failed due to losses within its investment portfolio. These losses were, in part, also absorbed by that corporate's member credit unions. In its testimony before the Senate's Committee on Banking, Housing, and Urban Affairs in 1995, the General Accounting Office reported that "NCUA's supervision of Cap Corp was ineffective on several fronts. For four years, NCUA essentially tolerated weaknesses in Cap Corp's internal controls; also, examiners who lacked investment expertise evaluated individual securities rather than securities portfolios."

Specific concerns reported to the Committee by GAO representatives included the finding that NCUA ". . . failed to take prompt action to correct clear weaknesses in Cap Corp's risk management system. NCUA not only let Cap Corp take on substantial investment risk without sufficient controls, it also failed to evaluate the risk of Cap Corp's entire portfolio or to reflect that risk in assigning CAMEL rations for Cap Corp." The GAO testimony also included the conclusion that "Had NCUA focused earlier on the overall portfolio decline and required proper recognition of losses in Cap Corp's financial results, the impending liquidity crisis might have been recognized earlier."

In closing comments, the GAO offered eight recommendations to NCUA. It should be noted that NCUA did, in fact, take steps to address most of these recommendations (including the recommendation to "increase the expertise of staff overseeing corporate credit unions"); however, there were two critical recommendations that NCUA ignored. The seeds of the current corporate credit union debacle can be seen in NCUA's failure to address these recommendations.

The first of these recommendations was to "Establish a tripwire system which would require prompt corrective action before a failing credit union's capital is exhausted."

Though subsequent regulatory revisions to Part 702 of NCUA's Rules and Regulations did address prompt correct actions a "natural-person" credit union (one of the 7,400) would be required to follow if its capital dropped below certain levels, the provisions for corporate credit unions contained in Part 704 were "window dressing" with overdependence on paid-in capital from the corporate credit unions' members. Therefore, NCUA's Regulations failed to impart a sense of urgency to corporate credit unions in regard to net worth growth and failed to provide adequate protection to the corporates' member credit unions. As a result, both risk and capital were not adequately addressed within the corporate credit union network.

The second is seen to be the more serious of the two. GAO recommended that NCUA

"Delay implementing any policy that would allow corporates to compete with each other for membership until necessary regulatory reforms, including adequate capital standards, are established and in force." Not only did NCUA not delay such implementation, the NCUA Board continued to aggressively approve national charters for corporates that significantly contributed to the on-going competition among corporate credit unions. This continued increase in competition among corporates for credit unions' deposits quickly led to the sacrifice of safety for yield – often for gains of only one or two basis points in yield. Over the intervening 15 years, the most competitive corporates chased yields into excessive credit concentrations, private mortgage based securities and their derivatives, CDOs, and other high-risk structured securities.

NCUA's on-going laissez faire approach to competition within an undercapitalized segment of the credit union movement is a significant contributing factor to the loss of as much as $13 billion by credit unions and their member/taxpayers as projected by NCUA.

### Lack of Accountability

Management at the failed corporate credit unions have paid and, for some, continue to pay a heavy price for their decisions and, in some cases, apparent neglect; however, the equally culpable professionals at NCUA have, to date, been untouched and have not yet been held accountable by Congress for their part in the corporate credit union losses. This disparity in accountability is unacceptable.

NCUA's Lack of Sound Budgetary Management

## NCUA's Budgetary Approach

At the same time credit unions are facing austere measures to meet the assessments levied by the NCUA, maintain positive earnings, and protect their reduced capital levels, the NCUA board has approved an operating budget for 2011, which includes a 12 percent ($24 million) increase over their 2010 budget. The 2011 budget increases include:

A five percent base salary increase for a significant number of NCUA employees with some staff receiving increases of up to eight percent. This is particularly galling considering the fact that the corporate losses have forced many credit unions to forego pay increases for their staffs over the last two years,

A two-year pay freeze is in effect for other agencies, and President Obama only approved a 1.4 percent increase for our military.

An overall 12 percent increase in total employee salaries and benefits.

The addition of questionable positions (within the current economic environment) including those in the Office of Minority and Women Inclusion, the Office of the Chief Economist, and the Office of Consumer Protection.

$2.5 million in capital acquisitions including $1.2 million for "continuing renovation of the Agency's 18-year old headquarters." $670 thousand to move the headquarters of the Agency's Capital Region. $555 thousand "for central office initiatives for replacing old furniture, painting, security and other minor building repairs and maintenance."

The 2011 budget increase follows a 13 percent increase in its 2010 budget, which included a less than helpful $2 million public relations campaign featuring Suze Orman.

*Shouldering the Cost*
NCUA and NCUSIF expenditures are paid by the nation's credit unions and their 91 million member/taxpayers through insurance premiums and assessments and add to the already burdensome $8.3 to $10.5 billion in charges being levied by NCUA as a result of the agency's failure to adequately fulfill its supervisory responsibilities.

The Durbin Amendment to the Dodd–Frank Wall Street Reform and Consumer Protection Act
The Dodd-Frank Wall Street Reform and Consumer Protection Act (Act) was signed into law by President Obama on July 21, 2010. The purpose of the Act was to "Restore responsibility and accountability in our financial system to give Americans confidence that there is a system in place that works for and protects them. We must create a sound foundation to grow the economy and create jobs." Shortly before passage by Congress, the Durbin Amendment was attached which requires the Federal Reserve to promulgate rules to regulate the US debit card market. On December 16, 2010, the Fed released their proposed rules. The US has the premier financial payment system in the world; however, these proposals, if enacted, will have material, long-reaching and adverse impact on the financial services industry, the nation's payment system, and the American citizens. It will not contribute to the stated purpose of the Act but will, in
actuality, work against this purpose.

*Debit Card Interchange Fees*

Among the requirements contained in this rule is a $0.12 hard cap on the per-transaction interchange fee charged by issuing institutions. Studies have shown that the median variable cost for a debit card issuer to perform a signature debit transaction is $0.175 based on a narrow definition of "allowable costs" and only variable costs at that. Actual per transaction costs are much higher than the calculation allowed by the draft Fed rule.

Though institutions with assets less than $10 billion are excluded, the market driven impact of this proposed Fed rule will rapidly encompass all financial institutions regardless of size, and both credit unions and community banks will not be immune. The impact on credit unions offering no-fee debit card services to their members will be significant with reductions in credit card-related revenue of as much as 75 percent. The result of this amendment will be a materially unprofitable debit card transaction service. The intent of the Durbin amendment was to reduce the fees vendors pay to the issuing financial institutions, which the vendors in turn would pass to the consumer through price reductions. It is very debatable whether this will be the result since the amendment contains no provision for such action by the merchant or any suggested framework to review and monitor the impact on merchants and their members/clients/customers. The overall impact on the consumer will, at best, be "breakeven" as financial institutions are forced to generate replacement revenues through the increase of current fees, the implementation of new consumer fees, and the reduction of benefits associated with debit card transactions. This will make the forced restructuring of the debit card market as well as the increased reliance on prepaid cards the Durbin Amendment's lasting consequences.

## *Issuer Participation*

A second issue, which the Fed is considering under the Durbin Amendment, is the question of issuer participation in debit card networks. The Fed is considering one of two potential rules:

• All debit cards must participate in at least two unaffiliated debit card networks. In all likelihood, this will mean one network for signature debit and a different unaffiliated network for PIN debit.

• All debit cards must be in at least two different networks for each authentication method (i.e., two networks for signature debit, and two networks for PIN debit). Regardless of which network rule is adopted, there will be significant operational upheaval and customer disruption for many issuers.

# Appendix B

Sarasota
Coastal
CREDIT UNION

The Growth
of Sarasota
Coastal Credit
Union Centering on the needs of the community,
credit unions are stronger than ever.

# Letter from the President

Sarasota Coastal Credit Union provides financial benefits to its members through lower loan rates, higher savings rates and fewer fees than banking institutions. Well, isn't that as boring as watching paint dry? We can demonstrate savings of $2,751,213 in direct financial benefits to our members for the period ending June 2007. Are you still awake?

Hi, my name is Tom Randle and I have been the president/CEO of Sarasota Coastal Credit Union since July 1989. My financial industry career began in 1970, so I am getting long in the tooth. However, that affords me a perspective on credit unions as they have emerged from their humble beginnings in the early 20th century to the age of instability in the emerging 21st century.

Today's credit union has to be able to reinvent itself, manage faster member response and implement faster technology innovation. Adaptation and anticipation are vital. We have to think quickly, strategically and creatively. With 100 years of history, credit unions have demonstrated that they are in a constant state of evolution.

Sarasota Coastal Credit Union began in 1953 and if you were asked, "A credit union is a kind of ____?," the response would be (1) a financial institution, or (2) a kind of bank. The problem with those answers are that while Sarasota Coastal Credit Union is a financial institution, it is not like any other, and the second answer that we are like a bank only applies to the services offered. We are very different in terms of the emotional experience of being a member.

Sarasota Coastal Credit Union is different. The following is the story of our history, values and people helping people mission. It is one thing to claim, "We have low loan rates," and it is another to tell you why. Sarasota Coastal Credit Union is a not-for-profit, financial cooperative. Because of that, we match our practices to our values.

We hope that as you gain familiarity, you will focus on our value proposition—members benefit financially and save money. Sarasota Coastal Credit Union has local management and the ability to make decisions and act quickly. Our field of membership provides access to the benefits of membership to all persons living or working in Manatee, Sarasota and Charlotte counties.

I invite you to leisurely enjoy this professionally developed narrative and share the story with others. We believe you will find it informative and compelling.

Sincerely,

**Tom Randle**

PRESIDENT/CEO

Original Bee Ridge Road office

> "Credit unions are
> economic democracies...
> At a credit union, every
> customer is both a
> member and an owner."

## Our Story

On December 12, 1953, seven school teachers with $130 and extraordinary foresight signed a Certificate of Organization to form a credit union in Sarasota. Today that credit union—Sarasota Coastal Credit Union—is still going strong with nearly 26,000 members. And the members aren't just members or customers—they're owners!

With other financial institutions faltering and even fading into the horizon, why has Sarasota Coastal been going strong for nearly 55 years? Like other traditional financial institutions, it can handle all of your banking needs—but you'll notice things are a bit different. Sarasota Coastal, like all credit unions, is a member-owned, not-for-profit cooperative with a volunteer board of directors. The focus of credit unions has always been to put members—not profits—first. Tom Randle, Sarasota Coastal's CEO/President, says "At a bank, the stockholders' interests center on maximizing the return on their investment. At your credit union, the interests center on the needs of the members."

**Membership-owned and Oriented**
Randle explains that a credit union—unlike a bank—is a not-for-profit cooperative financial institution that's owned and controlled by the members who use its services. All income that a credit union collects, after expenses and reserves, is distributed as dividends to its members. It's also used to provide competitive rates for loans, lower fees and more services. Credit unions are based on the concept of people helping people. "It's a cooperative," says Randle. "It just happens to be a financial cooperative. Sarasota Coastal is organized as a 501(c)(14), under IRS code."

"We're not stockholder-owned," notes Sam Murrow, Vice President of Sales. "We don't focus on quarterly profits. We're free to fight for the financial needs of our members, including the people who usually fall through the cracks: single working mothers, seniors on fixed incomes and undercapitalized, small business owners. Credit unions are economic democracies. Each member has equal ownership and one vote—regardless of how much money a member has on deposit. At a credit union, every customer is both a member and an owner." It's a brilliant concept. How did it all begin?

**A Progressive History**
America's first credit union was founded in 1908 in New Hampshire. The core idea was to create an alternative to the financial institutions of the day, where high interest rates and loan sharking were standard practice. In 1934, President Franklin D. Roosevelt signed the Federal Credit Union Act, forming a national system to charter and supervise federal credit unions. As a result, credit unions grew—and helped turn the bad times around.

John Delp, a 30-year member and current director, is proud of that history. "In 1935, when credit unions were helping Americans through the Great Depression, the treasurer of a Midwestern credit union said that credit unions were 'not for profit, not for charity, but for service.' That philosophy holds true today."

This people-first ideal helped credit unions grow steadily during the post-World War II boom years. By 1960, America's credit union membership totaled more than six million

~ 130 ~

people in more than 10,000 federal credit unions. Today, nearly 90 million Americans are members of a credit union and credit unions hold more than $615 billion in savings. In the greater Sarasota area, the history of the credit union is inseparable from the history of the educational community.

## Shoebox Beginnings

Darrel Wininger, a retired school teacher, current director and a member since the first year of inception, recalls the early years of struggle when the Sarasota County Teacher's Credit Union was formed. "Back then, we did all of our banking and business in John Wallace's extra bedroom." Wallace was the organization's first manager, he explains, chuckling as he recalls that Wallace kept the members' money in a shoebox. Eventually, this burgeoning enterprise outgrew the back bedroom. The few dozen charter members pooled their money and moved their corporate headquarters to a humble trailer on Hatton Street. It was an ideal location, close to most of Sarasota's schools.

From these modest beginnings, the enterprise grew into today's Sarasota Coastal Credit Union, an acclaimed institution with five branches serving nearly 26,000 individual and business members in Manatee, Sarasota and Charlotte counties. "We started out by helping the educational community," notes Ed Repulski, a founding member who has served on Sarasota Coastal's board of directors for more than 30 years. "Today, we help the whole community. That's the reason we changed our name." Despite its phenomenal growth, Sarasota Coastal's commitment to the credit union ideal has remained the same. Repulski sums it up in one word: "service." He adds, "Dedication to service is one more thing that sets us apart."

## People Helping People

Delp, an educator, remembers his first encounter with the credit union. When he and his wife arrived in Sarasota 30 years ago, they had less than $700 to their name. He was on his way to a job interview when his car gave up the ghost. "I went to several banks begging for a loan to tide us over before I got my first paycheck," says Delp. "They made me feel like a small fry—they didn't want my business. The only place that would loan us money was Sarasota Coastal Credit Union. Through all of these years, I've never forgotten this. When another young couple is going through tough times, I want to make sure they can find a place to get help. That place is Sarasota Coastal Credit Union."

"People helping people is more than a slogan, around here," notes James Dawson, Sarasota Coastal's board chairman. "We walk the talk." He says the credit union's commitment to service extends beyond its members. Its philanthropic partnerships include community organizations such as All Faiths Food Bank, Children's Haven, Sarasota Coalition on Substance Abuse, United Way, and the American Cancer Society. Additionally, Sarasota Coastal staff members make frequent presentations to local schools to share financial knowledge with students. Along with financial contributions, Sarasota Coastal is generous with its sweat equity.

"For years, Sarasota Coastal's management, staff and board members have been involved in painting houses for Brush Up

## SANDY ADCOCK
### Member Service Specialist

**There's a reason Sandy Adcock** has worked for Sarasota Coastal Credit Union for more than 25 years. "Before Sarasota Coastal, I worked at a so-called regular bank," she says. "I heard about credit unions and decided to apply for a job at this one. After the interview, I knew this is where I wanted to be." The difference? "I was warmed by the friendly atmosphere," she says. "I know it sounds like a cliché, but it feels like family here."

In her 25-plus years at Sarasota Coastal, Adcock has proudly served as Vice President of Lending and Vice President of Operations. For the past two years, she's worked as a Member Service Specialist—a position she's passionate about. "Our members aren't just numbers to us," she says. "We know their names and their children's names. They know ours. We care about their personal lives. When they thrive, we thrive."

Adcock has dozens of Sarasota Coastal anecdotes she keeps close to her heart. "There are so many success stories," she says. "We see people banks left behind—people no one else would help. When we're able to help them, we're all touched." She laughs, adding, "There are bank officers in the area with my card. When they're not able to help customers, they send them to me. Ninety-nine percent of the time, we're able to help them."

"Another Sarasota Coastal advantage? "We're very involved in the community—and that's important to me," Adcock says. "This is my community, after all—and I'm proud to work for a company that gives back to it."

Sarasota, selling cookbooks to benefit All Faiths Food Bank and mentoring at-risk students via the Big Brothers Big Sisters program," says Dawson. "We share the philosophy it is our responsibility and privilege to get out and do something good for the community we live and work in."

### The Difference That Counts

What's the best-kept secret about credit unions? Thanks to their not-for-profit status (credit unions pay all taxes except corporate income taxes), they can offer services at lower costs than consumer banks. They also charge lower interest rates on loans, including mortgages, so the savings go right into members' pockets. Whether it's providing a loan to help a member cover unexpected medical bills, giving financial counseling to new parents or simply offering a better deal on a car loan, the difference counts.

At Sarasota Coastal, everything comes back to its core mission: To provide a first-class experience, competitive pricing, convenient access and exceptional products and service to its members. "The member is our mission," says Sandy Adcock, a Member Service Specialist who's been with the credit union for 25 years. "As a Sarasota Coastal member, you have a voice and a vote. You're treated with respect and dignity. That's a breath of fresh air in this day and age."

"We get to know each other," she adds. "Our members aren't just numbers to us. We know their names. We're a part of their lives and they're a part of ours. We don't just push them through the lines. They're part of our family—and that makes all the difference."

Another longtime employee, Ernestine Anderson, echoes the sentiments of feeling like part of the family. "At Sarasota Coastal, we look at each person's circumstances and assist with their unique situations. We want to develop long-term relationships with each and every member."

### Green Isn't Just the Color of Money

In 2007, Sarasota Coastal Credit Union became the first financial institution to receive approval from the Sarasota Green Connection as an approved "green" business. It is also a certified Sarasota County Green Business Partner. Sarasota Coastal embraces the idea of reducing its impact on the environment. From recycling, reducing energy consumption and the volume of printed

materials, its employees believe everything can have a positive impact.

In fact, the credit union changed its service model, so that the majority of transactions that a member formerly had to travel to a branch to receive are available via telephone or Internet. By implementing secure technology, members no longer have to get into their cars and travel across town and go into the branch to apply for loans, open accounts or other services. Everything can be done via phone or email—how convenient! Documents are securely transmitted via Internet to a member's computer where they can choose to print any documents or simply save them to their own computer. Mike Boker, Vice President of Information Services says, "Members have embraced the new model as it saves them time and money. They are impressed with the level of security that the credit union provides for handling their transactions."

(L-R) John Sleaman, N. Lynn Kendall, Gail Shell-Mailer, Lee Fischer
Past Board Members

"We want to develop long-term relationships with each and every member."
*Ernestine Anderson*

### Vehicle Loans

Sarasota Coastal Credit Union is the regional leader in loans for new and used vehicles. "Our Auto Advisors program is acclaimed throughout the state," says Dawn Linthicum, a 20-year Sarasota Coastal employee. "Our advisors will not only find you the absolute exact car you want, they'll even deliver it right to your door." The program, Linthicum explains, partners with auto dealerships to provide a huge inventory of options. Bottom line? Sarasota Coastal's Auto Advisor service smoothes the ride on the way to buying a vehicle.

### Business Services

Sarasota Coastal empowers area entrepreneurs with a full range of business services and programs, including business savings and checking accounts, lines of credit, real estate loans, tax payment and payroll servic-

## JOHN E. DELP
### Immediate Past Chair, Sarasota Coastal Board of Directors

**John E. Delp's introduction** to Sarasota Coastal Credit Union took place 30 years ago when he and his wife first arrived in Sarasota with $700 to their name.

On Delp's first job interview, their car caught on fire. "We needed a few hundred dollars to fix the car but with rent and other moving expenses, we just didn't have it," says Delp. "I went around town with my hat in my hand, and every bank showed me to the door. I was just small fry to them."

Until, that is, he stopped at Sarasota Coastal. The Delps were given a loan that day and the rest is history. Soon after they settled in, Delp served on Sarasota Coastal's advisory board before moving on to serve on the board of directors. "After I earned my MBA, I felt I could help them even more," says Delp who, before retirement, spent his "days as an educator and my nights as a stockbroker. Whenever the opportunity arrives to help with something, I jump. I've never forgotten their trust in me."

Delp is proud of the way Sarasota Coastal has grown through the years. "But no matter how big we become, there's a whole different philosophy at work here," he says. "We are a cooperatively owned institution. We're all members and owners. There's a strong desire to help each other become successful." Bottom line? "When you walk through our doors, you're treated with respect," Delp says. "We don't believe in small fries."

Union can help you explore leasing options, streamline cash flow and even suggest options for developing a cost-effective, attractive benefits package.

### The Coastal Connection

Sarasota Coastal Credit Union members enjoy a host of state-of-the-art, services—from a courtesy pay program that covers overdrafts to streamlined online banking that offers members user-friendly access to all of their accounts, and the ability to pay bills and loans and manage their money online. SARA, its audio response system, allows the same ease of use for those who prefer the phone to the computer. For members who prefer doing their business in person, remote tellers speed up the deposit and withdrawal process—but still provide a friendly face to talk to. Drive up Sarasota Coastal members get the same courtesy. For greater access for members, there are five Sarasota Coastal branches: three in Sarasota, one in Venice and one in North Port.

Other financial benefits offered through a Sarasota Coastal membership include free checking, fewer transaction fees, special financing on auto loans, institutional credit cards with low rates and personalized banking solutions. Sarasota Coastal also offers members no-cost financial advice, including retirement planning, investment basics and real estate purchasing. Additional benefits include special credit union deals through partnerships, including an online travel site, laboratory and prescription services and identity theft protection. Behind all of the friendly faces and perks, though, there's solid business strategy at work, along with good, old-fashioned fiscal accountability.

es, employee pension programs and investment plans. "We understand the value that small businesses add to our community," says Randle. "Their success is everyone's success." Thanks to this commitment, more than 600 area businesses are Sarasota Coastal members. Other business services include state-of-the-art technology for online and telephone banking and bill paying, business money market accounts, merchant services, low minimum balances and monthly fees and specially trained business advisors.

"Managing your business in a volatile economy is a challenge but you don't have to go it alone," says Randle. The Business Services Team at Sarasota Coastal Credit

> "Our members become part of our family here at Sarasota Coastal."
>
> *Alma Hudson*

~ 133 ~

## Fiscal Accountability

Now, more than ever, credit unions are a safe harbor for consumers' money. Why? "We lend responsibly," says Sarasota Coastal CEO/President Tom Randle. "We always did and we always will. It's the credit union way."

"In the wake of the Lehman Bros. and Merrill Lynch debacles, many consumers are becoming more concerned about the financial soundness of their financial institutions," says Guy M. Hood, president and CEO of the Florida Credit Union League. "Where some financial institutions are reeling from the economy, credit unions are not."

It's not fuzzy logic. It's solid, down-to-earth business practice. Credit unions have been practicing this since their beginnings. Most credit unions are well capitalized with strong deposit growth. Their sound underwriting policies have sheltered them from the storm that has dismantled the world's large financial institutions. Just as banks around the world have tightened their lending standards, credit unions are able to create more lending opportunities and suffer less credit risk exposure.

"In 2008, mortgages at credit unions grew faster than all other loans," says Randle. "This at a time when mortgage losses have forced other lenders to scale back or close their doors entirely. We have continued to lend during this time through conservative underwriting. Unlike banks and brokers, we're not out to force loans on our members just to make a quick buck."

In today's economy, more people are turning to credit unions in order to put their money in a stable institution that offers good rates. "Our members saved nearly $3 million in direct financial benefits during the six months ending in June 2007, Randle says. "These benefits are equivalent to $111 per member or $211 per member household."

"Credit unions offer the best of both worlds," says Dawson. "They look out for their members' interests and provide a level of accountability and competitive pricing you rarely find at other financial institutions."

Across the nation, banks have been compensating for the losses of their easy-money credit spree and bad loans. They've been tightening liquidity and making it harder to get a loan. Credit unions have avoided dubious speculation—and exposure to risk. Credit unions don't need to tighten lending standards—their standards have always been

> "We use the latest technology to provide first-class service to our membership."
> *Mike Baker*

high. Their underwriting practices have always been sound. They haven't experienced the losses that banks have, so they're not undercapitalized. As a result, credit unions can still give out consumer and small business-friendly loans—after an intelligent and sound appraisal, of course.

It always comes back to the credit union philosophy: to empower members and the communities they live in. "We're a close knit group of people working for each other and want to see everybody advance," says Alma Hudson, a Member Account Specialist who has worked at Sarasota Coastal for more than 20 years.

"We started with seven people and our principles and guiding mission haven't changed since then," says Randle. "When you're ready to take control of your financial destiny, we invite you to become a member and discover the credit union difference!"

## ED REPULSKI
*Sarasota Coastal Board of Directors Member*

Ed Repulski's **Sarasota Coastal Credit Union** story sounds familiar. He and his wife moved to Sarasota in 1957. They were about to have a baby and in need of a small loan. A teacher and coach, Repulski went to the one place he knew he could find help. Back then it was called the Sarasota County Teacher's Credit Union. "In those days, the Credit Union was operated out of the manager's back bedroom," Repulski says. "That didn't matter. They conducted themselves with the same professional expertise, trust in their members and fiscal responsibility that still holds true today. The Credit Union slogan is 'People helping People.' We take that seriously."

Repulski was asked to serve on the supervisory committee and ultimately joined the board of directors, a role he has held for 30 years. He proudly refers to his 3-digit member number. "We now have nearly 26,000 members," he says. "It's a big and growing family—but the essential mission still remains strong."

That mission, he explains, is to provide the highest quality products and services to its members. Just as important? No one member is less vital than the other. "Back in 1957, I was made to feel significant, even though I didn't have a lot to my name," he says. "It's the same way today. Every member is a key part of this enterprise. Through good and bad times, that commitment has remained the same." It comes down to one single but powerful concept, he says. "People helping people."

~ 134 ~

# TIMELINE

- December 12, 1953
  Founding of the Sarasota County Teacher's Credit Union
- August 31, 1983
  Name changes to Sarasota Coastal Credit Union
- 1983
  Checking services offered
- July 1984
  Sarasota Coastal's Bee Ridge branch opened
- 1993
  Sarasota Coastal's original Fruitville branch opened
- September 29, 1993
  Membership is extended to all people who work and live in Sarasota County
- March 31, 1999
  Membership level at 23,800 people
- March 31, 1999
  Total assets at $105,500,000.00
- May 27, 1999
  Membership is extended to all people who work and live in Manatee and Charlotte counties
- August 2001
  Sarasota Coastal's Lakewood Ranch corporate offices opened
- April 2003
  Sarasota Coastal's current Fruitville branch opened
- March 2006
  Sarasota Coastal's North Port branch opened
- October 2006
  Sarasota Coastal's current Venice branch opened
- 2007
  Sarasota Coastal offers business accounts and services
- December 31, 2008
  Membership level at 25,566 people
- December 31, 2008
  Total assets at $224,335,548

## Locations

Contact all locations by calling (941) 907-4000
Mailing Address: P.O. Box 15407
Sarasota, FL 34277-1407

**Bee Ridge Branch**
3000 Bee Ridge Road
Sarasota FL 34239

**Venice Branch**
1485 E. Venice Avenue
Venice FL 34292

**Fruitville Road Branch**
5981 Fruitville Road
Sarasota FL 34232

**Parkway Collections Plaza**
6206 Lockwood Ridge Road
Sarasota FL 34243

**North Port Branch**
2467 Sycamore Street
(off Toledo Blade Blvd. between I-75 and Price)
North Port, FL 34289

1st location at State and Halton

# About the Author

Tom Randle served the credit union movement for twenty-nine years and served as CEO, Sarasota Coastal Credit Union from 1989 to 2009. He was employed with ITT Aetna Finance for ten years before beginning his credit union career. He is a US Army Vietnam veteran.

He has served on the Board of Directors of the Credit Union Executives Society (CUES), was the Chairman of the Board and elected to the CUES Hall of Fame. Tom was a member of the inaugural class to earn the designation of Certified Chief Executive (CCE). At that time, Tom was the first person elected via a petition to rise to Chair, CUES.

He earned the designation of Certified Credit Union Executive (CCUE) and a Bachelor of Arts degree in business. He is a Credit Union Development Educator.

Tom is past chair of the Sarasota Coalition on Substance Abuse and its 2010 citizen of the year, past Secretary of the

Florida Credit Union League (FCUL), past director of the Florida Credit Union Shared Services, past trustee of the Florida CU Foundation, and a past member of the FCUL Legislative Affairs Committee. He served as a director, Big Brothers Big Sisters of the Suncoast, and as its governance committee chair. He was a BBBS mentor to high school students in a dropout prevention program. He is a court appointed special advocate (CASA) in Georgia and is the chair, NE Georgia CASA board of directors.

He has practiced yoga for years and began teaching about 3 years ago. If he is not at yoga, he may be found at CrossFit, hiking, or golfing.

Since moving to Georgia, he has been active in his church where he is a ruling elder, and served on the boards of County Chamber of Commerce and the Convention & Visitors Bureau. He was active in Rotary for years.

He earned the designation of Certified Business Coach and founded KES Group LLC in 2010 to develop leaders, team building and executive strategic planning.

He has been happily married for 31 out of 47 years, the father of two and two granddaughters. He is a mediocre golfer.

He also loves to connect with readers. You can connect with him on:

**Website:** https://kesgroupllc.net/

**Blog:** http://www.kesgroupllc.com/blog/

**Facebook:** https://www.facebook.com/tomrandlejr

**Twitter:** https://twitter.com/mtncoach

**Instagram:** https://www.instagram.com/tomrandle5r

**LinkedIn:** https://www.linkedin.com/in/tomrandle

# Acknowledgments

As is always the case, I did not do this alone and there are people to thank.

D. D. Scott, my editor, writing coach and chief encourager.

Quite a few others who provided stories and quotes used.

The Redhead, my wife and confidant, who turned down the television and gave me space to complete this project.

And all the wonderful people with whom I had the honor and privilege to lead.

# Books by Tom Randle

*Shouldering the Cost: One Credit Union CEO's Take on the Great Banking Collapse of 2008*

*Knowledge Plus Execution Equals Success: 21 Lessons to Make Positive Behavioral Changes in Yourself, Your Team and Your Organization* --- Coming Soon!

# Excerpt from Tom Randle's Next Book

**Knowledge Plus Execution Equals Success: 21 Lessons to Make Positive Behavioral Changes in Yourself, Your Team and Your Organization**

It is my hope that you, and your organization, will take the lessons in this book and use them as a launching pad. If that stimulates a conversation, or is an impulse for positive behavioral change in you, or your organization and your team, my job is done.

There are millions of references to leadership on the Internet, and tens of thousands of books on the subject. You have read some, and probably forgotten most. Successful leaders are life-long learners and demonstrate a thirst for information, especially if that data helps them achieve the vision and mission of their organization.

That is why I want to present useful information, supported by real work experiences and application, and do so in a brief format, based on many of the blogs and articles I've written over the years.

Leadership of others begins with leadership of self. You cannot truly become an effective leader of an organization until you identify leadership on a personal level.

After service in the U.S. Army, including a tour in Vietnam, I began a financial services career that spanned 39 years. I was blessed with a career that provided me with opportunities to experience more than most. I have travelled the globe and worked with wonderful people at several different organizations. It was my singular honor to have been surrounded by and supported by persons of integrity, honor and intelligence. Our disagreements were usually gracious, collaborative and useful.

We all live in a hectic world. There are demands on our time. We struggle with work-life balance. And, when it comes to leadership and culture in our organizations, we don't talk about it enough.

Take the lessons I'm sharing with you and use them. There is one per business day. The power of spaced repetition (reading new information five or six times) can result in a 62% retention rate after fifteen years. To get the maximum reward, I challenge you and your team to read each lesson 5 to 6 times.

Everyone has time to do that. Get copies for your management team and make it required reading. Form a discussion group at staff meetings. If you want different results…DO SOMETHING DIFERENT!

My mission is to see you make more money, enjoy a work-life balance and be successful.

Life is wonderful. Do something great with yours.

www.ingramcontent.com/pod-product-compliance
Lightning Source LLC
Chambersburg PA
CBHW071309220526
45468CB00001B/310